Gender Politics in Transition. Women's political rights in Egypt after the
January 25 Revolution.

To my family and
to all women of the Arab revolutions

claudia ruta

TABLE OF CONTENTS	
ABBREVIATIONS	6
GLOSSARY	8
I. INTRODUCTION	11
1.1 Research problem, objectives and hypothesis	12
1.2 Academic and social relevance of the research	15
1.3 Methodology and structure of the field work analysis	18
1.4 Book structure	26
II. NATIONAL LIBERATIONS, ENGENDERED TRANSITIONS & DEMOCRATIC DEMANDS: A CENTURY OF WOMEN'S ACTIVISM IN EGYPT AND ABROAD	27
PART ONE	
2.1 The case of *Maghreb*: women in Algeria and Morocco between resistance and liberation	29
2.2 The quiet revolt of Iranian women under the Islamic Republic	34
2.3 The successful model of South Africa: the women's movement and the gendered political struggle for democracy	37
2.4 Politicizing feminism in Chile: the transition to democracy after Pinochet's regime	41
2.5 Sub-conclusion	44
PART TWO	
2.1 Early signs of women activism in the Arab world: the reformist resurgence	47
2.2 1919: Egyptian women between national-activism and political segregation	49
2.3 From Nasser to Sadat: women's rights amidst Pan-arabism and *infitah*	54
2.4 Women's rights during Mubarak's time	60
2.5 Sub-conclusion	66
III. WOMEN AMIDST POLITICAL ACTIVISM, AND THE TRANSFORMATIONS OF POST-MUBARAK EGYPT	68
3.1 The awakening of Arab dignity: the case of Egypt, triggers, and causes	69
3.2 A modern *thawra*: the making of a revolution	73
3.3 Taking to the streets: 2011 like 1919	77
3.4 Women & politics in the transition: missing the gains of the revolution	81
3.6 Blacking to old Egypt: the case of gender-based	98

coalitions and groups	
3.7 An emerging force: women of the Muslim Brotherhood	103
3.8 Suzanne Mubarak like Jihan Sadat: clashes over the Personal Status Laws	109
3.9 Sub-conclusion	116
IV. EGYPTIANS SPEAK: SOCIAL PERSPECTIVES ON WOMEN'S RIGHTS IN THE POLITICAL TRANSITION	118
4.1 Results of the empirical study	119
4.1.1 Egyptians on women's participation in the revolution	120
4.1.2 Women and Tahrir square: reflecting on March 8	122
4.1.3 Can women lead in Egypt? An analysis	124
4.1.4 Maintaining or abolishing the quota system in Parliament	130
4.1.5 A social reading of Egyptian feminist groups	132
4.1.6 Debating the Personal Status Laws: the *khul'*, the custody law, and the legal age of marriage	136
4.1.7 Political Islam: perceptions of the Muslim Brothers and the Salafist movement	139
4.2 Addressing women's social difficulties and their causes	141
4.3 Quick notes on personal observations of the focus group discussions	144
4.4 Sub-conclusion	147
V. CONCLUDING ANALYSIS	149
5.1 Feminist activism and its impasse: reasons and lessons learned	149
5.2 After January 25th: which revolution for women?	155
5.3 The unchanged nature of the Egyptian society	159
5.4 A new beginning?	163
5.5 Need of further research	166

REFERENCES	168
LIST OF APPENDIXES	200
Appendix I: Chronology of major events	213
Appendix II: Groups and women's movement formed after the revolution	218
Appendix III: Egyptian's Women Charter	222
Appendix IV: List of interviewed experts	227
Appendix V: Topics discussed during the semi-structured interviews	228
Appendix VI: Survey results & figures	
LIST OF TABLES	
Table n. 1: Interview participants	22
Table n. 2: Respondents Focus-group 1	23
Table n. 3: Respondents Focus-group 2	23
Table n. 4: Respondents Focus-group 3	23
Table n. 5: Family Focus-group 4	24

ABBREVIATIONS

AAW	Alliance for Arab Women
ACT	Appropriate Communication Techniques for Development
ADEW	The Association for Development and Enhancement of Women
ANC	African National Congress
AWSA	Arab Women Solidarity Association
BWA	Bureau of Women's Affairs
CEDAW	Convention on the Elimination of All Forms of Discrimination Against Women
CEWLA	Center for Egyptian Women's Legal Assistance
CSO	Civil Society Organizations
ECWR	Egyptian Center for Women's Rights
EFU	Egyptian Feminist Union
FEDTRAW	Federation of Transvaal Women
FIS	Islamic Salvation Front
FLN	National Liberation Front
FMG	Female Genital Mutilation
GDP	Gross Domestic Product
IAEA	International Atomic Energy Agency
ICPD	International Conference on Population and

	Development
IMF	International Monetary Fund
IRC	Al-Azhar Islamic Research Centre
MB	Muslim Brotherhood
MDG	Millennium Development Goal
MENA	Middle East and North Africa
MP	Member of Parliament
MWS	Muslim Women Society
NCCM	National Council for Childhood and Motherhood
NCW	National Council for Women
NDP	National Democratic Party
NGOs	Non-Governmental Organizations
NOW	Natal Organization of Women
NWF	New Woman Foundation
PBUH	Peace Be Upon Him
SCAF	Supreme Council of the Armed Forces
SERNAM	National Service for Women
SNM	National Secretariat for Women
UN	United Nations
UNFA	National Union of Algerian Women
UN Women	United Nations entity for Gender Equality and the Empowerment of Women
UWO	United Women's Organization in the Western Cape
VAW	Violence Against Women
WNC	Women's National Coalition
WTO	World Trade organization
WWCC	Wafdist Women's Central Committee

GLOSSARY

Abaya: it is a robe-like dress usually black which covers the whole body except the face, feet, and hands. It is the typical dress of women in the Arabian Peninsula.

Dawa: preaching Islam and spreading the message of the *Qur'an* and the worship of God.

Fatwa: legal opinions related to the Islamic faith and Islamic law issued by the Mufti.

Hadana: the wife's right to remain in the conjugal home during the period of child custody.

Hadith: the record of Prophet Mohammed's sayings (PBUH) which all together constitute the *Sunnah. Hadiths* and the *Qur'an* are considered the sources of the Islamic law, the *Shari'a.*

Hanafi: the largest of the four schools (*madhahib*) of religious jurisprudence in Sunni Islam. It is now predominant among Sunni Muslims in Egypt and Pakistan. Followed by 30 percent of Muslims worldwide, it is considered to be the most liberal.

Haram: something prohibited under the *Shari'a.* Its antonym is *halal* (permitted).

Hijab: is the common veil worn by Muslim women. It has different shapes and colors.

Fitrah: term developed by Sayyed Qutb to distinguish about women and men's roles. Because of their *fitrah,* women are more compatible with the role of caretaker.

Ijtihad: a personal effort, independent of any school of jurisprudence, to interpret Islamic law. By the end of the 10th century, theologians decided to close the doors of the *ijtihad* to solidify Islamic theology and free interpretation.

Infitah: introduced by Sadat it was a liberal policy which encouraged foreign investments in the country, privatization and the end of the state control over national companies.

Jellabeya: traditional Egyptian tunic mainly used by men.

Jihad: struggle in the name of God; holy war. There are different kinds of jihad: an internal struggle to maintain faith, the struggle to improve the Muslim society, or the struggle to defend Islam.

Khalifa: the head of state or the ruler of the Islamic *Ummah*. After the death of Prophet Mohammed, the community has been guided by four *Khalifa*.

Khul' (**no-fault divorce**): The possibility for women to file for a no-fault divorce was introduced in January 2000 by a decree from President Hosni Mubarak. The law grants Egyptian women the right to ask for divorce without requiring them to provide evidence of harm or to find witnesses. However, women filing for *khul'* are required to forfeit their rights to alimony and their deferred dowry (*mu'akhar*) and to repay their advanced dowry (*muqaddam*).

Majlis al-Shaab: People's Assembly in Egypt, the lower house of the bicameral Parliament.

Majlis al-Shura: the Upper House of the Egyptian bicameral Parliament. The lower house is the People's Assembly.

Maquis: remote mountainous areas from which Algerian fighters launched the struggle for independence against the French in 1954.

Moujahidats: women heroines who participated in the fight for independence in Algeria.

Niqab: is a cloth for women that covers the face and let only the eyes visible.

Shari'a: Literally translated as the "right way or the path," it includes the body of laws based on the *Qur'an* and the *Sunnah* of the Prophet. It regulates the public and other aspects of Muslims' private life. It covers many aspects of daily life, such as economics, business, politics, sexuality, criminal law, marriage laws, and of course, religious observances.

Tafsir: the science which aims to make clear the true meaning of the *Qur'an*, its injunctions, and the occasions of its revelation. The *tafsir* developed into a system of systematic exegesis of the *Qur'an*, and it has been employed by Islamic reformists in order to articulate a modern interpretation of the *Qur'anic* text.

Tagammu': leftist progressive unionist political party.

Takhayyur: in Islamic jurisprudence, it means choosing legal rules from a variety of sources.

Thawra: literally means "revolution" in Arabic.

Ulema: a scholar of Islamic law and religious leader.

Ummah: the Muslim community or people belonging to the religion of Islam all around the world.

Wafd: created in the 1920s, it is still a prominent nationalist and liberal party in Egypt.

CHAPTER I

INTRODUCTION

This work is about the development of women's political roles and rights before and after the revolution of January 25. It will adopt Gramsci's hegemonic theory to identify the power game played between the Egyptian state and women's groups at the time of the three presidents and in the current post-Mubarak transitional period. It will investigate to what extent the state is willing to include women in national politics in its run toward democracy, and how secular women's groups (including NGOs)[1] will mobilize to counter-balance the hegemonic discourse and to succeed in improving women's political representation in the transitional government. Besides, this work, through an empirical study, will aim at underlying Egyptians' views on gender politics at large.

1.1 Research problem, objectives, and hypothesis

The strong participation of women in the Egyptian revolution of January 25, which started to put an end to Mubarak's regime, offers a significant insight for studying the progression or decline of women's social and political rights in the current transition. Questions surrounding modern-day women's activism became especially interesting in light of the current political situation. It became increasingly difficult to ignore the role that women have played during the revolution and their apparent exclusion from any type of political consultations and reforms. After having analyzed the roles that women have played in revolution struggles or independence movements in Algeria, Morocco, Iran, South Africa, and Chile, and the strategies adopted by women to be included politically in the transitional[2] and post-transitional periods, this work will consider in detail the case of Egypt and the relations between the state and women's groups in terms of the complex interplay of power and hegemony. Despite the active participation of women in the independence struggle of 1919, and the early efforts of feminist groups in Egypt between the '20s and the '40s, improvement of women's political and civil rights has been limited during the century. After the independence from British colonialism, women's support was no longer seen by male politicians as useful and women's rights were not included in the secular legislation and policies of the state (Badran 2009, 32; Mariscotti 2008, 38). Despite the different political orientations at the time of the three presidents, with the adoption of socialism first and liberalism then, women's political participation has always lagged behind the level of rights recognized in the Constitution and the laws regarding women. Furthermore, because of the power struggle played between the state and a resurgent conservative Islamism, social relations in the family were left unaltered and women were left subordinated within the patriarchal structure of the family.[3] Women's rights have been exploited to counter-balance the commanding discourse of conservative Islam as a tool to reach the ends of the state in terms of consolidating its ideological hegemony (Karam 1998, 23). According to Gramsci's theory of hegemonic power[4], the state struggled against women to both maintain and to gain political power and hegemony. Hence, for Egyptian women's groups, the issue has been that of counter-balancing gender subordination to the state's discourse and certain conservative Islamic groups while seeking alternative ways of social and political engagement (Karam 1998, 24). But without strategic alliances with influential political constituencies, women's groups' commitment to redefining gender roles remained marginal. Furthermore, because of the social belonging of these groups, it seemed to the Egyptian population that those who were calling for political rights were only secular women, not representatives of the majority of the female population. As Nawal El Sadawi said in this regard: "The women's movement kept away from an active involvement in the national and political life of the country, and limited its activities to charitable and social welfare work" (Baker 1998, 274). The Egyptian state has consequently promoted specific roles for women for pragmatic and ideological reasons upholding unequal gender relations by making authority out of political convenience. While the state did not independently give power to women, women failed to become strongly politically engaged.

Thus, this work, by taking the revolution as turning point and by analyzing current governmental policies toward women's political inclusion and social attitudes about women's rights, will try to identify the current relations of power between the state and women's groups. Various forms of women's political and civil activism will be studied by looking at the actions of old and new women's groups, how they have adjusted their demands, where they are heading, and which successes and/or problems they are currently facing.

The aim of this work is threefold. First, through a literature review and theoretical framework, I have set out to understand the development of the women's movement in Egypt in terms of its relations with state power and patriarchal discourse. This will be done by thinking back over the steps and the features of women's groups at the time of Nasser, Sadat, and Mubarak. Secondly, the book will look at the participation of women in the revolution of January 25, post-regime state policies and women's groups adopted strategies to face the political challenges of the transition. Indeed, this study aims at taking a close look at the political participation of women, seen as a launching pad for reshaping and consolidating social equality in Egypt. Third, through an empirical study targeting Egyptian men and women, the book will provide data on themes related to gender politics and women's political rights in the country. Looking at the available literature, central questions are formulated as follows:

1. What is new in women's activism compared to the past in the way women's groups are struggling for political inclusion against male hegemonic power and social patriarchy?

2. To what extent is the Egyptian's transition including women in the political transformations after the January 25 revolution?

3. What experiences can be drawn from the other countries in order for women to succeed in their request of

political representation?

4. To what extent have Egyptians modified attitudes and social visions in relation to women's political rights and roles?

Through empirical and secondary literature research and by taking into consideration theories of power and an in-depth comparative analysis of the impact of previous transitional periods in Middle Eastern countries as well as the South African and Chilean experiences, and their post-polities, this work argues that for women's political rights to progress and for women to achieve a role in the transitional politics, women's groups and activists should engage politically in strong constituencies through visible presence in the streets, assimilating their requests to Egypt's democratic ones in order to express their demands in a manner of social justice. In order for women to be politically accepted, it will be fundamental, in this critical period, to equate women's requests to the broader cause of social justice and democratization to avoid labeling women's demands primarily as gender-driven. Egypt needs good women politicians who are not *porte-parole* of feminism but true leaders of everyone. As Badran ha recently said, there is a need of a "new feminism embedded in revolution." This new feminism should announce itself from the core values of the revolution, maintaining its spirit while redefining its identity according to social demands of freedom, liberation, justice, dignity, democracy, and equality (Badran 2011). Only in doing so will women succeed in making sure that gender issues will actually be translated into positive gender outcomes in the post-transition period.

1.2 Academic and social relevance of the research

The Arab revolutions and the current political transitions of the Middle East are new and absolute extraordinary phenomena and mark a turning point in the history of the world. As a political science researcher, I found it an unconditional duty to study and analyze the current political transformations in Egypt, which, along those of Tunisia, have started the whole process.[5] The Egyptian revolution and the public participation of women in the protest movement is an important issue that should be investigated in order to understand what is really changing in the country, at the dawn of the process of democratization, in terms of gender politics and democratic rights.

The topic of representative democracy and women's political participation is indeed considered one of the most important political subjects that has increased in significance since the end of the last century and has attracted numerous researchers and politicians among those concerned with the matter of the political participation of women. However, there are still few academic discussions that deal with gender dynamics in transition to democracy and in consolidation of the new political institutions (Seidman 1999, 302). Today, any serious study or research pertaining to political transition and electoral legislations cannot fail to put forth this matter (Soufi 2009, 252). As Soufi also states, democratic systems cannot be implemented without solving the matter of the deficiency of female representation or its complete absence altogether in certain instances (Ibid, 253).

There exists a growing body of scholarly literature on the feminist movement in Egypt, mainly in terms of differences between its secular and Islamist wings (Ahmed 1992, Badran 1996, 2009; Baron 1994, 2005; Botman 1999; Karam 1998; Mariscotti 2008; Nelson 1996). Because of the novelty of the situation, this work seeks to contribute to the body of already existing research by examining the ongoing events, identifying the current path of relations between state and women, investigating the latest strategies of women groups, and looking at how women's issues are now included in the current political debate. In addition, this work will also examine the issue through an empirical study in order to combine literature review and field work observation, which, to my knowledge, very few have done before. In fact, except for a some research that, through interviews, has addressed members of the feminist movement, there has not yet been any serious scientific attempt made to analyze how ordinary Egyptians are experiencing not only the current events, but how they view women's involvement in political actions, the Personal Status Laws, the rise of Islamist groups, the feminist movement, and its effects upon public debate in the country.

Hence, by exploring the issue of women's participation in politics, it will be possible to evaluate the stage of political transformations toward which Egypt is progressing. It has been proved that development cannot be achieved without giving women rights and new instruments to empower themselves. Hence, it becomes necessary to focus particularly on improving women's political participation as a milestone on the way for Egypt to social and political modernization (Mustafa, Shukor and Rabi' 2005, 28). As Inglehart and Norris also argue in an interesting revision of Huntington's theory on the "Clash of Civilizations," gender equality is becoming the main indicator for judging the democratic status of a state (Rizzo, Abdel-Latif, Meyer 2007, 1152). Catherine Warricks also adds that gender issues have assumed a high relevance in the theory of political science. Gender is currently much more than a subcategory of politics, but it has a symbolic and functional significance across a wide variety of political issues (Warrick 2009, 179).

1.3 Methodology and structure of the field work analysis

The bibliographic review of this work has been developed with consideration of diverse kinds of materials. During the days of the revolution and immediately after, I have looked at YouTube videos, articles, and Facebook groups in order to have a preliminary understanding of women's activism during the days of the revolt. In the time between February and August, I have been researching and collecting not merely books and journal articles but also conference proceedings, bloggers' posts and newspaper articles from the main Egyptian publications. This research has been considerately all-inclusive in order to propose an accurate chronologic representation of the events in question. Various press releases, petitions, and statements prepared by Egyptian women's groups and NGOs developed during and after the revolution have been also a source of analysis. Since my project aims to show the links between wider political culture and women's activism, I have also examined different academic as well as non-academic sources that deal with Egyptian politics. While newspaper articles, websites, etc., proved to be useful to observe and describe the current events, the book review mainly served as background study in order to propose a comparative analysis on the political involvement of women in worldwide revolutions and the social and political implications for women's rights following the end of these conflicts. Besides, the review has been useful to introduce the historical role of the Egyptian state and the changing policies under Nasser, Sadat and Mubarak and state's relations with women's groups. Among others, I looked to several scholars like Ahmed 1992, Badran 1996, 2009; Baron 1994, 2005; Botman 1999; Karam 1998; Mariscotti 2008; Nelson 1996; and Sullivan 1986 in order to compare and contrast the current implications with past history. Finally, a group of work that I am constantly referring to provides an analysis of the evolution of the legal system from the 1920s, when the first Personal Status Laws were codified, until the most recent reforms. This group of texts investigates the status of women under the Islamic *Shari'a* and their rights in matters of divorce, marriage, custody, maintenance, testimony, and inheritance (Al Alami and Hinchcliffe 1996; Arabi 2001; Bernard-Maugiron 2010; Haddad, Yazbeck and Esposito 1998; Moussa 2006; Naveh 2001; Paonessa 2000; Zantout 2006).

The field work for this book was developed during the months of June and July, and it has followed a triangulated approach. In preparation to that, I conducted a daily analysis and scrutiny of printed and online media, and monitored Facebook. I developed my research through a multi-method research plan including qualitative (semi-structured interviews and focus groups) and quantitative (survey) analysis, and combined bibliographic and field research. In conducting focus group discussions, I have relied on a combination of personal observation and open-ended questions.

In this research, triangulation served to capture a more accurate, *holistic*, and contextual portrayal of the participants in the study. It also serves to validate the findings of the other methods used: "In this sense, triangulation may be used not only to examine the same phenomenon from multiple perspectives but also to enrich our understanding by allowing for new or deeper dimensions to emerge." Besides, "the effectiveness of triangulation rests on the premise that the weaknesses in each single method will be compensated by the counter-balancing strengths of another" (Jick 1979, 603-604). Indeed, the use of a triangulated research strategy is not only aimed at confirming the validity of the research, but at deepening and widening the understanding of the political and social phenomenon being investigated. The mixing of methodologies, like the use of survey data with interviews, is the most profound form of triangulation (Olsen 2004, 1-3; Tellis, 1997).

The use of an empirical study also provided a complete exploration of the phenomenon in question, going beyond the experimental or quantitative research in order to give the researcher up completely to the real-life phenomenon (Tellis, 1997). Qualitative research allows for a more in-depth description and explanation of the issue in its social context, represented through the voices of the actors involved. These findings cannot be stated as statistical evidence as they represent subjective perceptions that do not necessarily reflect the researcher's point of view (Duthie 2004, 3).

This work has mainly targeted two groups of interest. The first is composed by women activists, media experts, Muslim Brotherhood members, Islamic law experts, and academics, for a total of twenty-two people interviewed.[6] Different kinds of experts were included in this study in order to provide a good representation of the topics in question. These interviews, following the Leech categorization of "elite interviews" as respondents, can be categorized as experts about the topic at hand and can be treated as such (Leech 2002, 663). The scope of these semi-structured interviews has not been that of homogenizing the different kinds of respondents targeted, but of offering an in-depth account of those movements involved in the process. Interviews also had a more conversational quality than highly structured interviews, allowing for a deeper investigation of the reality being researched. Furthermore, in order to explore the feelings, ideas, and experiences of the average Egyptian, the field work relied on a empirical study of ordinary people composed of seventeen semi-structured interviews, three focus groups, one family focus group discussion, and one survey.

The field-work conducted among ordinary Egyptians has, however, only targeted literate people. Even though this work recognizes the anthropological and ethnographic studies conducted by Diane Singerman 1996 and Lila Abu-Lughod 2008 and their analysis of gender relations within scarcely educated and poor communities, this research, however, has adopted a conceptual research framework which would exclude illiterate people as target of analysis. Doing field-work with illiterate people would indeed require the application of certain anthropological approaches which go beyond the scope of this research.

The participants of the in-depth interviews were also mainly recruited using the snowball technique.[7] The first participants in the study shared with me the names of friends, relatives, neighbors, or colleagues that I might contact for further discussions. As for the in-depth interviews, the group consisted of eight men and nine women.[8] Most of the interviews lasted between twenty minutes to an hour and were held face-to-face in a café or at their homes. In only one case, interview was conducted by telephone. I really appreciated the Egyptian sense of collaboration and enthusiasm with this work. On several occasions, many Egyptians opened the doors of their homes, inviting me to speak about my research without fearing the interference of a foreign student in their private lives. It has been a combination of humanity and hospitality. Being a foreigner made possible for me to interview people from different social classes and level of education because I stood outside the Egyptian social hierarchy and political affiliations. All interviews and focus group discussions were recorded and transcribed immediately after.[9] For recording information, I also used a field diary to collect records about observations and analytical notes. Most of the interviews were conducted in Arabic with the assistance of a mother-tongue researcher who helped me on some occasions, working as an Arabic interpreter. In other circumstances, I managed to do interviews even in French and Italian. The translations of interviews and texts that appear in the work are mine. Some researchers helped me with the translation/transcription of Arabic interview types. In writing up the quotations, I have kept the written text as close to the original as possible.

Table n.1 Interview participants

Resp. No	Name	Age	Education	Gender	Job
1	Fares	28	Degree in Commerce- CU	M	Counter clerk
2	Adam	57	Degree in Literature	M	Director of TV educational program
3	Mervat	32	Degree in Psychiatry -ASU	F	Psychiatrist
4	Doria	30	Degree in Medicine-ASU	F	General Doctor
5	Amir	21	Student of Physical Therapy-CU	M	No
6	Fareeda A.	21	Degree in Foreign Languages-ASU	F	Freelance interpreter
7	Mariam	20	Student of Tourism-CU	F	No
8	Salma	57	Degree in Literature-CU	F	Writer and teacher
9	Farah	32	Student of Law-ASU	F	Lecturer
10	Mohmena	44	Degree In Literature-CU	F	School director
11	Ahmed A.	20	Degree in Commerce-CU	M	Oracle developer
12	Monir	26	Degree in Electronic Engineering-CU	M	Computer engineer

13	Marien	40s		F	French teacher
14	Zaneti	35	High school diploma	M	Taxi driver
15	Zen	39	Degree of Arts-CU	M	Theater director
16	Reem	41	Degree in Translation-AZU	F	Teacher
17	Ahmed B.	30	Degree in Journalism-AZU	M	Teacher

*CU: Cairo University   ASU: Ain Shams University   AZU: Azhar University
AUC: American University in Cairo   HU: Helwan University
*No stands for those that are still enrolled in a university programme while unemployed for those that have graduated.

In addition, three focus groups were held in order to explore in detail some of the issues elaborated upon individually during the interviews.[10] The first group discussion consisted of five persons and was held in my home (Table 2). The second one consisted of six participants and was held at the Cairo Opera House café' (Table 3). The third focus group consisted of four persons and again was held in my home (Table 4). These three focus groups lasted about an hour and half. The family discussion, which happened during a Thursday night family gathering, lasted around forty minutes. All participants to these focus groups were contacted using the snowball sampling technique, and they varied in age between twenty and sixty years old. All the findings show similar conclusions, and thus they have been analyzed in a combined manner. A study with this population of participants enabled me to draw conclusions on the common perceptions of women's political involvement in the revolution, women's rights and gender roles, *Shari'a* law, patterns of equality in family laws, and common perceptions of women's participation in the public sphere and in positions of leadership. Similar perceptions have been also tested through an online questionnaire.

Table n.2 Respondents Focus Group 1

Resp. No.	Name	Age	Education	Gender	Job
1	Mohammed A.	29	Degree in Law-CU	M	Lawyer
2	Mahmoud A.	30	Degree in Media Press-AZU	M	English teacher
3	Leila	31	Degree in Economics-ASU	F	Online Teacher and translator
4	Somaya	26	Degree in International relations-American University of Beirut	F	Works at NGO
5	Nuran	24	Student of Political Science-	F	Government employee

			AUC		

Table n.3 Respondents Focus Group 2

Resp. No.	Name	Age	Education	Gender	Job
1	Fareeda B.	20	Student at Alsun-ASU	F	No
2	Suzanne	20	Student at Alsun-ASU	F	No
3	Mohammed B.	24	Degree in Tourism and hospitality-HU	M	Tour guide
4	Samy	26	Degree in Commerce-CU	M	Unemployed
5	Sayyed	21	Degree in Arts-HU	M	Unemployed
6	Ahmed C.	19	Student of Arts-HU	M	No

Table n.4 Respondents Focus Group 3

Resp. No.	Name	Age	Education	Gender	Job
1	Khaled	28	Degree in Law-CU	M	Lawyer
2	Magdi	22	Student of Medicine-CU	M	No
3	Mahmoud B.	21	Student of Medicine-CU	M	No
4	Islam	27	MA in Media-AZU	M	Imam

Table n.5 Family Focus Group

Resp. No.	Name	Age	Education	Gender	Job
1	Imen	20	Student of Engineering-CU	F	No
2	Menna	27	Degree in Computer Science-CU	F	Computer Programmer
3	Sarah	40s	Commercial Institute	F	Housewife
4	Marwa	40s	Degree in Commerce-CU	F	Government employee
5	Abrar	37	Bachelor Degree	F	Housewife

Because of the triangulated technique adopted, and in order to verify data collected through the qualitative analysis, a survey with both closed and open questions was carried out between mid-July and mid-August. Quantitative methods like survey research can make important contributions to field work in the ability to generalize results (Jick 1979, 604). The survey was written in Arabic, published online, and spread using social networks like Facebook and Twitter. Thus, it should be noted that this survey only targeted members of the lower-middle and middle-upper class, and those who possess a computer and an Internet connection. However, some members of the lower-middle class were also reached through interviews and focus groups, making the research socially inclusive. Survey's respondents were targeted using both the snowball and random sample approaches. The high number of answers was sufficient to avoid the hand-by-hand recruitment. In total, 139 respondents between the age of seventeen and sixty years participated in the survey (sixty-two women, seventy-seven men). The majority of the respondents were youth between twenty and thirty years old, mainly with undergraduate university degrees and living in Cairo.

This particular research also took ethical issues into utmost consideration. At first, all participants were briefed about the goal of the research and informed that their names and details will not be shown. Moreover, I was obliged to protect the subjects by trying to minimize disturbances both to subjects themselves and to the subjects' relationships with their political environment and to politically sensitive issues (Social Research Association 2003, 35). To protect participants' identities, pseudonyms have been used and quotations used from interviews and focus groups do not identify the participants. Data concerning gender, age, education, and socio-economic background of the participants do not reveal the identities of the subjects and have been consequently left unaltered. This is with the exception of experts, who have agreed on having their names and titles included. This research also followed other ethical principles. First, it was important to establish an egalitarian and horizontal relationship between myself and the research subjects in order to relate with the participants in a friendly way, leaving behind in some occasions the formal researcher-informant relationship. As Shrader and Sagor argue, "guaranteeing confidentiality of the information is not a theoretical ideal: it is an absolute necessity for carrying the study" (Shrader and Sagor 2000, 94).

This research also produced a huge quantity of data. However, in the analysis, some of the data has been omitted due to spatial limitations, leading to a simplification of the respondents' stories.[11] While presenting personal stories, I had to decide, at some point, which aspects to include and exclude; research can never be entirely objective, and social research is not an exception. Besides, the selection of topics and questions may reflect a certain bias in favor of certain cultural or personal values. Hence, confidence in research findings depends critically on their faithful representation (Social Research Association 2003, 24). Finally, it should also be noted that participants in this study also represents a minimal segment of the entire Egyptian population and that results cannot be generalized. Indeed, the research sample being quite small, and data for the most part non-numerical, it is impossible to establish the probability of which the results are representative of the larger population.

1.4 Book structure

The book consists of three central chapters, plus an introductory and a final chapter dedicated to a concluding analysis. The second chapter is divided in two parts and introduces a comparative analysis of the topic in question by studying the role of women during worldwide revolutions, the aftermath of the new political setting for women's rights and the strategies adopted by national women's groups to deal with the post-regime state policies and including women's demands in political reconstruction. The chapter also reports the historical perspective of the feminist movement in Egypt, proposing in so doing a chronological reconstruction of the events. The third chapter proposes a timeline of the major events happened during and after the recent Egyptian revolution regarding women political participation, social activism and state politics about women in the current political transition. This chapter will be built upon interviews conducted with the experts which will be the leading voices of the narrative. The fourth chapter represents a lively depiction of the facts analyzed, in the case through the lens of average Egyptians who will comment and debate the current themes of discussions relevant to the recent political involvement of women. Finally, the concluding chapter is dedicated to a final wrap-up of the main ideas produced in this work as well as the final analysis of the results of the case-study work by proposing an accurate theoretical and political interpretation of the events.

CHAPTER II

NATIONAL LIBERATIONS, ENGENDERED TRANSITIONS & DEMOCRATIC DEMANDS: A CENTURY OF WOMEN'S ACTIVISM IN EGYPT AND ABROAD

Studies of international relations have occasionally focused their attention on the roles played by women in transitional periods, and their political outcomes for women's rights. In several cases, indeed, during wars of independence or revolutions, women have played a key role in the breakdown of authoritarian regimes. Even though many of the promises of the earlier phase have rarely been fulfilled and women have been often disillusioned with the subsequent outcomes, they fought to engender the political transitions of their countries, making sure that women's rights were recognized and included in the new structures of the state (Waylen 2010, 337). Thus, in order to understand the development of the Egyptian female activism and its involvement in state politics during the century, it is useful to engage at first in a comparative analysis with other Middle Eastern and foreign countries in order to analyze similarities and differences with the current case.

The chapter describes women's engagement in revolutionary or independent movements in five countries leaving the analysis of Egypt to the second part of this chapter. The revolutions and post-periods that we will be examining closer are Algeria's 1962 post-colonial revolution until the civil war, Morocco's battle against French colonialism and its aftermath, women's rights after the formation of the Islamic Republic of Iran and the strategies adopted by its movement, the South African experience and the politicization of the women's movement there and its successes, and finally the Chilean case at the time of General Pinochet.[12] This investigation will elucidate how women's movements have been engaged in political transformations before, during, and after periods of transitions; to what extent they have been successful in leading to the progression of women's rights; and the strategies they have adopted to engender the political change.

Therefore, this chapter will first aim to explore the realities of the women's movement at an international level, the best strategies and the achieved successes; second, it will travel over the history of the Egyptian feminism in order to link past circumstances with the current post-revolution events.

PART ONE

2.1 The case of *Maghreb*: women in Algeria and Morocco between resistance and liberation

Frantz Fanon's description of Algerian women's participation in the war for independence from France (1954-1962) is memorable. Algeria's history is full of events and actions conducted by women in the political domain; the example of Lalla Fatma N'soumer is enlightening, as it reflects the path of a female leader who guided a male army and the resistance against the

French army for several years in Kabylie.

As soon as the war of independence broke out in 1954, women entered the battle, and around 10,949 of them became active participants in the independence revolution, 3.1 percent of all those taking part in the fighting (Amrane-Minne and Abu-Haidar 1999, 63). Women of all ages participated in the revolution, some directly involved even in fighting in the *maquis* (rebel forces operating in the mountains) (Knauss 1987, 75-77). Algerian women were not merely sympathizers or militants on a short-term basis, but real fighters who joined the National Liberation Army or the Civil Organization of the National Liberation Front (Amrane-Minne and Abu-Haidar 1999, 62-63). Women also were committed to other tasks as organizers, arms transporters, guides, and nurses, because they could be easily mistaken for normal civilians (Ibid., 65). About 2,200 women were tortured by the French forces and police (Turshen 2002, 891).

Algeria won independence in 1962, and women secured equality in the constitution and in citizenship rights, as well as access to education, health services, and professions. However, along with independence, Algerian women found the promises of the socialist revolution unrealized. National freedom did not bring women's enfranchisement in Algeria (Cooke 1989, 2). When all those who had fought in the war for independence were convened to discuss the new state, women were badly represented. As one woman combatant said: "Our domestication didn't start in 1962, it happened before independence; even during war, the National Liberation Front (FLN) started eliminating women from the *maquis*, sending us to the borders or abroad. That's when our role was defined, when we were excluded from public life" (Turshen 2002, 893). During the first post-war meeting of the National Assembly, only ten women were invited out of the 194 members (Amrane-Minne and Abu-Haidar 1999, 69). In spite of the important role that they played in the liberation struggle and in the post-colonial reconstruction, Algerian women were immediately pushed into the background with respect to the participation in decision-making and laws regarding personal status.

Following the independence, the founding members of the National Union of the Algerian Women (UNFA) developed a charter that articulated women's demands and women's desired social roles and family responsibilities. Despite the fact that the UNFA soon became the "women's auxiliary" of the FLN in 1968, this did not increase women's political roles and participation in the political process. The state of the post-revolution presented an "atavistic response to the colonial legacy", starting with repressing women and restoring a social code founded on patriarchal principles (Knauss 1987, 137). In spite of President Ben Bella's intermittent declarations of support toward the woman's cause, society remained highly patriarchal. The emergency nature of women's participation in the revolution called afterward for a return to the "tranquility" of pre-war family life (Ibid., 95-96). At the time of the socialist military regime of Boumedienne, women continued to be ousted from the political arena; no women served on the Party's Central Committee, and not one was appointed to the National Council of the Revolution. Only in 1977 were nine women appointed to the National Popular Assembly (Ibid., 109).

In order to justify their claims and their right to political participation, feminists have always referred to the great role played by women during the Algerian independence struggle. However, the *moujahidats*, the heroines of the resistance, never affiliated themselves with the feminist movement, its elite or demands, and did not support any feminist political agenda. For the *moujahidats*, independence meant victory against colonialism, liberation, and a better life (Baker 1998, 275).

Only in the early '80s, women's groups started to organize in protest against a family code that would legalize the inferior status of women in family matters. The women's movement started a strategy of confrontation of the government by public acts of civil disobedience, and participated in several demonstrations. The largest national petition campaign against the code got one million signatures (Turshen 2002, 894). Women's groups succeeded in their struggle for reforms, and in 1982, the adjustment of the Family Code was suspended. However, in 1984, Benjedid's government deceived the women's movement once again by adopting a family code extremely repressive of women's rights. Women experts were not consulted during the intra-governmental discussion for the new code. The code made women inferior in education, work, divorce, marriage, and inheritance. The reason behind this choice can be found in the government's desire to appease Islamic conservative groups in the wake of a renewed politicized Islam after the Iranian revolution (Knauss, 125). Moreover, the women's movement remained also substantially urban and composed of middle-class women, and it rarely succeeded in putting down roots among rural women (Ibid., 137-138). Only in 1987, when a law was passed authorizing the creation of women's NGOs, did women start to systematically organize themselves in development associations (Turshen 895).

Algerian women reached the top of their social annihilation during the civil war of the 1990s, an epoch described by Klialida Messaoudi as "crimes against women" (Turshen 2002, 894; Knauss 1987, xiii). Once again, women remained the oppressed of the oppressed, used during the civil war as targets and pledges in the power struggle between the Islamists and the government (Turshen 2002, 897). The Islamic Salvation Front (FIS) proposed two *fatwas*, one legalizing the killing of unveiled women, and the second legalizing kidnapping and temporary marriages; thousands of women also became "war booty" (Ibid., 898). Algerian women took the streets several times against the FIS, courageously marching in protest every March 8. In 1995, women were the first to vote in the presidential elections despite the FIS call for boycott (Ibid., 902). As with the war of independence, during the civil war, the courage of Algerian women at the forefront of demonstrations became a symbol of social resistance.

In Morocco during the battle against French colonialism,

the revolt of women is what Australian literary critic Michael Hall has termed a "double rebellion" against colonialist occupation and oppression and the restrictive attitudes of the conservative society (Baker 1998, 3). During the independence movement, poor women from a growing neo-proletariat were among the leaders of the rebellion. When the events passed, Mohamed V shut out women leaders of the armed resistance. Those who had lost their husbands or divorced found themselves relegated to the margins of social life. Nationalist women, on the contrary, became an active part of the post-independence movement, and their public requests were made possible thanks to the support of the political male actors such as individual thinkers, the monarch, and members of political parties. Most of the nationalist women belonged to the middle and upper classes and had an influential male parent in the *Istiqlal*, which was the most popular party of the time (Sadiqi and Ennaji 2006, 96). While ordinary women who were active combatants of the resistance went back to their domestic roles, nationalist women got leading roles in education or social services (Baker 1998, 6). Members of the first group were not recognized and rewarded for the great contributions they had made in the struggle for national liberation; the shock was significant for those who discovered not much had changed in the society at large after independence—especially in regard to their rights (Ibid., 10).

Monarchy and kin-based sociopolitical groups emerged out of the colonial period willing to negotiate the structure and the orientation of the new state. The new alliance was reaffirmed to the detriment of women's rights and women's social and personal status. In order to safeguard the alliance with the tribal areas, the monarchy protected the patriarchal nature of the country (Charrad 2001, 147-148). The preservation of the family's vision as represented in the *Maliki* School of Law avoided disrupting kin-based solidarities and sought to maintain the social and political status quo. The force of *Malikism* was to permit the control of women by their male relatives and to protect the cohesiveness of patrilineages. Women who were not involved in the codification process of the Family Law Code found themselves put in a position of inferiority in the family. However, at that time, no public debate followed, and nationalist women simply ignored the issue because for them, family rights were not a priority (Baker 1998, 32).

Only at the end of the '90s did the women's movement start to be unified, and women's issues were finally open to public discussion and debate. Women's groups got the support of King Mohammed VI, who in 2003 pushed for the adoption of a new family law that significantly improved the status of women. Following this first step, in the following years, the king also appointed several women to political and high-profile positions. In 2002, thirty seats were reserved for women in Parliament during the national elections. These victories greatly boosted the feminist movement in Morocco, which succeeded in introducing gender issues in the national dialogue and public sphere, becoming a powerful agent of change (Sadiqi and Ennaji 2006, 105). From the beginning of the new century, the Moroccan feminist movement started to be compacted, "becoming an essential social and political actor and tool of democratization" (Ibid., 104).

2.2 The quiet revolt of Iranian women under the Islamic Republic

In Iran during the course of the twentieth century, women have been used as "footballs" in the cynical power games played between different political forces (Afkhami and Friedl 1994, x). The White Revolution removed Iranian women from the category of minors, granting them several rights, including the chance to exercise political power; women's enfranchisement in the Pahlavi period boosted the states' image through a well-constructed "democratic" façade (Ibid, 11). For the first time in their history, Iranian women found their space in the Parliament, the cabinet, legal professions, and family rights.

Women played an instrumental role in the success of the initial protests against the shah that took place in 1978 and 1979, using family gatherings and religious classes to spread information among the revolutionaries. When the revolutionary struggle was gaining momentum, Khomeini encouraged women to come out into the streets and join the demonstrations. Women of different backgrounds and political orientations participated in non-violent actions. Some of them took also part in guerrilla activities; a typical image prevalent throughout the revolution was that of the *khwahar-I mujahid* (warrior sisters). Despite the fact that during the revolution, women were not demanding women's rights *per se*, they believed that the Islamic revolution would take into account their position in society (Nashat 1983, 109). The emphasis was based on the consolidation of national sentiments rather than feminist or class-based ones (Ibid., 162). Besides, Khomeini's famous statements, such as the one saying "any nation that has women like the Iranian women will surely be victorious," allowed woman to interpret these remarks in a encouraging way (Ibid., 118). Khomeini was smart in mobilizing women, calling for their political participation and encouraging them to vote for the constitution in 1979 (Halper 2005, 108). The "woman question" became soon strictly interlinked with the construction of an Islamic national identity. Indeed, "the significance of women for the success and legitimization of the revolution included the promotion of an Islamic heritage that would revive an identification of society's moral and ethical values with virtuous women as the bearers of cultural purity and authenticity" (Sedghi 2007, 206).

In a few months after the end of Reza Pahlavi's reign, the newly established Islamic Republic called for the restoration of what was considered the primary role of women in society: a domestic one. Now that women had helped to establish a true Islamic government, they were kindly requested to leave the affairs of the state to men and concentrate on the social requirements requested to them by the Islamic *Shari'a.* Western models and lifestyles were banned, and conservative dressing started to be enforced by official decree. The *hijab* became connected to a sign of women's belief in the revolution and a rejection of imperialism and Western cultural models. However, early in 1979, on March 8, some unveiled women from the middle and upper classes marched in Tehran, demonstrating against Khomeini's statement on women's dress. A small demonstration became a protest rally, as some 15,000 women joined the march (Hoodfar 1999).

Women also attempted to form the Women's Solidarity Committee, a coalition of women's organizations intended to coordinate women's responses on gender issues. But the idea failed due to political divergences among the participants. Ideological and political differences among secular and conservative women remained strong, making impossible the realization of cohesive movement (Ibid). Besides, many traditional middle-class and poor women welcomed the return to the *hijab* as a sign of cultural heritage and a way forward toward a new Islamic modernism (Nashat 1983, 199). The public presence of secular women articulating liberal demands helped those Islamist women to express themselves within a well-accepted "Islamic" perspective, appearing as an "authentic" movement to the eyes of the political leaders of Islamic Republic (Hoodfar 1999).

In the following years, the Islamic Republic abrogated the laws it considered contrary to the *Shari'a,* which resulted in a drastic backlash of women's personal, political, cultural, legal, and social rights. Women started to be treated unequally under family rights; women's ability to seek divorce was restricted, as well as their right to custody of children. The legal age of marriage dropped from sixteen to nine, and temporary marriages were legalized (Nashat 1983, 208). Women could not be members of the Guardian Council or become part of political/religious institutions such as the Assembly of Experts. Between 1979 and 1986, women's employment decreased tremendously, and some 25 percent of the female workforce left the job market (Aman 2009). Most of the women working in public service sectors were also expelled because of their appearance and femininity (Mohammadi 2007, 2). Women were forbidden to work as judges, as in the case of Shirin Ebadi, the first female judge and winner of the 2003 Nobel Prize, who was forced to resign from her position immediately after the revolution (Aman 2009).

Beyond the social and political restrictions of the Islamic Republic, women increased their public militancy, engaging in what Bayat has defined as a "power presence." Contesting the *hijab* on a daily basis, women continued to make a power claim (Sedghi 2007, 264). Iranian women decided to combat a silent resistance against discrimination and patriarchy through ordinary daily practices of life, such as playing sport; they also used education as a cultural weapon, strongly increasing their presence at university level (Bayat 2009, 98). Despite its leaderlessness and scattering, because of its ordinary nature, this movement became irrepressible, and women succeeded in maintaining a visible position in society (Ibid., 111). Women also made great use of the print media, bringing gender issues directly to the public and openly exposing the discriminations suffered by women (Hoodfar 1999).

Women's conditions definitely improved under Mohammed Khatami, who called for greater social freedom. In the local elections of 2003, the number of female candidates increased by 60 percent; during his presidency, women also started to hold deputy minister positions, and women's presence in the educational and legal spheres was encouraged (Aman 2009). The Bureau of Women's Affairs (BWA), which reports directly to the president, also helped women express their criticism at higher level (Hoodfar 1999). The democratic opening of Khatami reinforced the women's movement and gave them self-esteem and the will to mobilize through NGOs and charities (Bayat 2009, 101). The number of women's NGOs increased between 1997 and 2000; they became successful in changing some of the family laws by lobbying through their few representatives in Parliament (Mohammadi 2007, 16). In 2007, the then-minister of interior, Ali Kordan, accused women's groups of being a security threat to the Islamic Republic (Aman 2009). However, the repeated attacks to the movement from the conservative clerics demonstrated the growing visibility of women's NGOs and their strength as a powerful social pressure group in Iran; besides, the ranks of the movement have been increasing in the past few years, and the trend is expanding outside Tehran (Ibid).

The recent Green Revolution confirmed this tendency and a growing social interest for women's issues. The national movement fighting against Ahmadinejad demonstrated to be far more sympathetic to the cause of Iranian women, realizing that without an equally empowered female counterpart, no political success can be achieved.

2.3 The successful model of South Africa: the women's movement and the gendered political struggle for democracy

South African women have been a source of inspiration for their active struggle throughout the course of the twentieth century. In 1948, the Afrikaner National Party launched apartheid, the most offensive system of racial discrimination. During that time, South African society was extremely patriarchal; women were seen as inferior beings, relegated to domestic roles and excluded from public matters. Women faced legislative discrimination in the Personal Status Code as all laws were based on the subordination of women to the males of the family. However, during the apartheid, South African women expressed their political aims by joining political parties and by being involved in the general struggle of the trade unions and civic organizations. Women were encouraged to fight apartheid alongside men rather than address concerns specific to women; any gender-specific activism was considered detrimental to the movement (Mihindou 2006, 29).

At the beginning of the '70s, with the apartheid system still enduring, women entered into politics in large numbers by participating in local political organizations. Three women's organizations were established, the United Women's Organization in the Western Cape (UWO), the Federation of Transvaal Women (FEDTRAW), and the Natal Organization of Women (NOW), and they succeeded in establishing strong political alliances and civil networks. These organizations, by working side-by-side with political actors, civic organizations and trade unions at grassroots level, became fundamental partners in the anti-apartheid movement, giving to the women's movement a successful strategic direction (Hassim 2006, 49). Over the years, women continued to stress the centrality of gender equality in the achievement of a democratic state. Thus, early in 1991, all parties agreed to introduce a Gender Advisory Board to ensure gender equality while negotiating agreements (Seidman 1999, 292-293).

Unlike the case of many African and Middle Eastern countries, the struggle against the apartheid and the following transition resulted in a major political role guaranteed to women and their inclusion in the representative government, constitutional drafting, and policymaking process (Hassim 2002, 693). At the beginning of the transitional period, women activists consolidated themselves in one unique, independent, and organized coalition, the Women's National Coalition (WNC), which was successful in introducing the notion of gender equality within the African National Congress (ANC)[13], a key negotiating force (Ibid., 694). Despite the fact that the coalition comprised seventy organizations and other regional coalitions, without the strategic alliance with the ANC, it would not have been so successful. The organizations differed in size, ideology, and organizational culture, and few were characterized by feminist demands. The ANC took a formal commitment toward women's rights, giving gender equality a special importance in the democratic process and voicing women's requests in national politics. "The existence of a strong political party that favored a structural transformation rather than merely a transfer of power and that, as a result of a slow process of internal trans-formation of decision-making processes and representational structures, had committed itself to eradicating gender inequal-ities, was a crucial factor" (Ibid., 696). Hence the great influen-tial role that the WNC had to mainstream gender equality in the public political discourse strongly depended on its link to pol-itical parties and not just on the strength of the women's move-ment (Ibid., 721). The WNC achieved what no women's group could have ever achieved on its own. It represented a wide var-iety of women; it had good organizational capacity and facili-tated a triple alliance of key women activists, academics, and politicians of all races (Hassim, 2006 in Waylen 2010, 340). In the election campaign of 1994, all political parties adopted cer-tain gender rhetoric; an activist even said that "gender con-sciousness has become one of the national priorities in South Africa" (Seidman 1999, 294). The concept of equality in citizen-ship rights as the new political ideal based on the respect of sub-ordinated groups in society, allowed women to articulate their claims for civil and political parity (Hassim 2002, 723-725). During the consolidation of democracy, the achievement of gendered citizenship also became one of the goals of the gov-ernment of Mandela.

In 1994, the new Parliament included 106 women, 26.5 per-cent out of 400 representatives (Seidman 1999, 288; 300). Four women were appointed as ministers and eight as deputy minis-ters in the cabinet. They were not only assigned to soft minis-tries, but they became deputy ministers of the finance and trade and industry portfolios (Hassim 2006, 185). Women were also elected to eighty of the 400 seats in the National Assembly, the only directly elected house of Parliament, and a woman, Frene Ginwala, was elected speaker of the National Assembly. Women also were elected to almost one-third of the seats in the nine provincial assemblies.

One important achievement also consisted in the development of a charter that formed the basis of the demands of the WNC in the constitutional negotiations, giving strong credibility to the articulation of women's demands[14] (Hassim 2002, 708). Besides, the WNC also pushed for the introduction of the non-sexism clause in the constitution, which was not spelled clearly in its first draft. "The uniqueness of the WNC's ability to lobby political organizations and demand a place at the negotiation table, while at the same time retaining its political independence, gave women a powerful voice at a crucial moment in South Africa's political history" (Ibid., 728). The South African Constitution became one of the most advanced democratic instruments in the world, including gender equality as one of the main principle of the new state (Waylen 2007, 161).

Recently, the role of WNC has started to diminish, and the space of advocacy for gender equality has been taken by NGOs and the Commission on Gender Equality, whose role is that of pressuring political parties and ministries about gender equality. Although in later years, the National Women's Machinery suffered from bureaucratic and financial difficulties, the leading political role women had before and after the apartheid became an example model worldwide for all women's movements struggling during transitional periods.

2.4 Politicizing feminism in Chile: the transition to democracy after Pinochet's regime

Women played important, though too often unrecognized or under-acknowledged, roles in all of Latin America's democratization processes; their participation in diverse movements during these democratization processes *in itself* proved transformational for the those involved.

In Chile, on September 11, 1973, General Augusto Pinochet Ugarte through a military *coup d'état* ended one of the oldest democracies in South America. The socialist government of Salvador Allende was overthrown with the strong support of the masses, and Chilean women had been among those fighting Allende's government more than the others. Economic hardships dictated by socialist policies and their detrimental implications for the well-being of the families were important factors that brought women to support the coup (Dandavati 1992, 52). Allende took power in 1970, despite women's massive support of the Christian Democrats (Supplee in Tétreault 1994, 394). Chilean socialism soon failed to recognize the important role that women might play; women, instead of being politically and socially mobilized, remained relegated to the margins of public life. Patriarchism, with its stress on women's domestic roles, remained intact. Indeed, "the socialist government casted its appeal in class terms but in gender ones" (Ibid., 401). The education system improved, giving women the opportunity to participate in public life but without assuring any advance of their social status (Ibid., 394).

After the coup, Pinochet promised to reward those women who had been sustaining his victory. A National Secretariat for Women (SNM) was immediately created, acknowledging women's new prominence in national politics. However, in terms of political representation and space in society, the conditions of women worsened. Pinochet stressed that the most important labor for women is motherhood and being the defender of the home (Waylen 2007, 54). Women's reproductive capabilities were once again manipulated as a means of domination (Dandavati 1992, 60). The National Secretariat, which was composed by wives of members of the armed forces and volunteers, assumed the role of protecting a social status quo according to which women's assignment was that of protecting the family and restoring women to the tranquility of the home (Supplee 1994, 406-407; Waylen 2007, 54). The Secretariat underlined that its objectives were to "highlight the importance of the woman and to cooperate in increasing her ability to better discharge the role of mother, spouse, and housewife" (Dandavati 1992, 68). Furthermore, women also lacked all kinds of legal rights to their children as well as any personal possession except for their salary. Women also became the first victims of the regime, tortured and raped because of their relations with men of the socialist opposition to Pinochet. In 2004, it was reported that around 12 percent of the Chilean torture victims were women, almost all of whom had been victims of sexual violence (Waylen 2007, 55).

Several types of women's organizations developed in response to the brutality of Pinochet's regime. The women's movement was mainly composed of human rights organizations, popular movements, and feminist organizations. Human rights women's groups united themselves around the *Agrupación de Familiares de Detenidos-Desaparicidos,* fighting for the release of relatives who were detained and/or victims of sexual violence. The popular urban movements were formed more by women who were pressing for social and economic demands by organizing campaigns for improving services and survival strategies (Waylen 1994, 336). Finally, feminist-only organizations focused their battle against patriarchism, gender divisions, and women's social subordination. Many feminists also joined political organizations, becoming activists in the opposition parties of the "renovated Left" (40 percent of the activists of the left parties' coalition *Concertación* were women)[15] (Waylen 2007, 124). However, because women continued to be located at the bottom of parties' ranks, and very few of them were selected as candidates, a number of independent feminists and women from political parties formed an alliance—the women's *Concertación de la Mujeres por la Democracia,* established in 1988 (Waylen 2010, 339). The aims of the alliance were to place women's problems on the national scene by enhancing women's role in politics, formulating a program for women's rights in view of the coming democracy, and ensuring gender commitments within parties (Ibid., 341). Because of the combined efforts of women from several political parties, *Concertación* became a successful instrument for pushing women's demands in the new electoral process (Waylen 2007, 76). It succeeded in improving women's legal position to incorporate women's demands in the political system and pushed for the adoption of a national machinery, the *Servicio Nacional de la Mujer* (SERNAM), which was established in 1990. In 1989, for the first time, women succeeded in having their demands recognized in the manifesto of the winning center-left coalition. That same year, seven women were elected to Parliament (5.8 percent of 120 deputies). This number increased to nine women in 1993 (8 percent) and thirteen women in 1997 (10.8 percent). Women have also had some success introducing quotas for internal party positions (Waylen 2000, 782).

The strategies adopted in Chile were successful because Chilean feminists started to believe that maintaining autonomous feminist movements was not going to get them anywhere in the changing circumstances. Chilean activists succeeded in pushing for gender equality more within the frame of political participation, than ideological separation while maintaining a strong social dimension (Waylen 2007, 102). Women demonstrated that they were able to unify action, in an effective political manner, and ready to challenge the status quo (Dandavati 1992, 131). The women's movement did not have the unique goal of removing Pinochet from power, but also a desire to alter social relations and to create a democratic and egalitarian society (Dandavati 1992, 119). The democratic path followed by Chile was once again confirmed in 2005 with the election of a woman for president, Michelle Bachelet.

2.5 Sub-conclusion

If we compare the history of Algeria, Morocco, and Iran, we notice how women's roles in revolutionary movements and transitional changes have been similar. While Morocco and Algeria were French colonies, Iran also submitted to a sort of indirect Western imperialism. In the case of Morocco and Algeria, nationalist movements mobilized women during the independence struggle, calling for their public participation. But with the end of the colonization period, the national political forces wanted to re-assert an identity based on local culture and religion, and on women's primary role as caretakers and guardian of the tradition. Thus, with independence, women gained very few civil rights, maintaining instead an unchanged subordinate position within the family. In all these cases, women were mobilized to advance the interests of the state and its liberation without receiving any kinds of reward for their trouble. In Morocco, the government's desire to appease Islamic conservative groups left unmodified the patriarchal nature of the country. In Algeria, the socialist government that took power after the independence in 1962 continued to perpetuate women's relegation to secondary roles (Baker 1998, 273). As Baker clearly explains, "the male political leaders who had consciously mobilized women to participate in the struggle for independence now just as consciously put them back into their accustomed place." In Iran, this step happened even more aggressively, when women, after having participated in the struggle against the shah, found themselves deprived of any judicial and civil rights and personal freedoms (Ibid., 274). Morocco and Algeria did not develop strong women's movements until the 1960s and 1970s, when these countries experienced a revival of feminist movements and a new pressure on women's subordination within the family, as well as economic and social issues affecting women. The Islamic Republic of Iran is a case *per se*, where, for several years, women have been fighting a sort of passive revolution by simply remaining visible on the public sphere.

Another case is that of South Africa, where the transition to democracy has been fairly easy for women, who have been included in the realm of representative government and whose rights have been assured in the new constitution (Hassim 2006, 129). In South Africa, the women's movement started to fight for gender equality and for political recognition early on by creating political alliances with sympathetic insiders in the political system across class and party lines (Ibid., 15). Moreover, at the beginning of the transitional period, women activists were successful in consolidating themselves in one unique, independent, and organized coalition, and in creating strategic alliances with the strongest political actor of the time, the African National Congress (ANC). Specifically in South Africa, the mainstream of gender equality in the public political discourse strongly depended on the link between the women's movement and political parties, and on the strength of the Women's National Coalition as a successful political entity (Hassim 2002, 721). In Chile as well, women activists joined leftist political parties in the transition. Because of the combined efforts of women from several political parties, *Concertación*, the winning center-left coalition, became a successful instrument in pushing for women's demands in the new electoral process (Waylen 2007, 76). Women's groups succeeded in pushing for gender equality more within the frame of political participation than ideological separation while maintaining a strong social dimension (Waylen 2007, 102).

Hence, the successful cases of South Africa and Chile demonstrate how the existence of autonomous women's movements is necessary but not sufficient for achieving women's substantive representation and the struggle for gender equality should be also fought with the support of at least one political organization active in the negotiations (Hassim 2006, 130). As both Hassim and Waylen have underlined, positive political opportunities and successful strategies adopted by the South African and Chilean movements have been crucial in differentiating the gender outcomes of these countries from those of Algeria, Morocco, and Iran.

PART TWO

2.1 Early signs of women's activism in the Arab world: the reformist resurgence

In the Arab world, early signs of women's activism go back to Prophet Mohammed's era (PBUH) and revelation of the religion of Islam. With the advent of Islam, women started to have a leading public role within the community of believers. Several prophetic *hadiths* and other oral stories narrate the social and political engagement of the prophet's wives as leaders of prayers, decision-makers, and pioneers in commercial activities. The religion of Islam granted women more and new rights in the fields of political participation, inheritance, and freedom of expression. Among others, prominent women were Khadija, a well-known merchant and first wife of the prophet; Aisha, consulted by men for her knowledge in theology and law and a strong combatant; and Um Salama, known for her curiosity and interest in knowledge (Hassan, Nasr and Morsy 2009, 32; Hussein 1953, 442). Between the end of the nineteenth century and the beginning of the twentieth, a first characterization of feminist ideology appeared, combined with modernity and Islamic reformism. As the historian and Islamicist Thomas Philipp argues: "The debate over the emancipation of women originated among Muslim reformists. They felt that the position of women had suffered, not through the commands of original Islam, but by a misinterpretation of the *Qura'n* and later un-Islamic additions" (Philipp in Sullivan 1986, 26).

The pioneer of the reformist movement was Rifa'a el-Tahtawi (1801-1873), who emphasized the principle of *takhyayyur*, the necessity to refer to the other school of laws to find solutions to modern matters when it seems it is most appropriate (Esposito 2001, 50; Arabi 2001, 186). He believed that although the rules of *Shari'a* are everlasting, their interpretations in terms of social conventions might be modified according to the times (Sullivan 1986, 27). Reformists Muhammed 'Abduh (1849-1905) and Jamal Al-Din Al-Afghani (1838-1897) also supported women's cause, calling for a new role for women much more in accordance with the changes of the time. They asked for increasing women's access to education and limiting men's unilateral right to divorce and polygamous marriage, among other demands (Mariscotti 2008, 3). 'Abduh also confronted the problem of patriarchal excesses committed in the name of Islam (Badran 2009, 20).

However, it was Qasim Amin (1863-1908) who became the real founder of feminist belief in Egypt and father of the modern women's movement and activism. Amin, a nationalist and intellectual, believed in the liberation of women as a launching pad from which to develop a free, advanced, and independent Egypt. Amin linked the deteriorating status of society to the low conditions of women, arguing, "We hope the Egyptian woman achieves high status through the appropriate avenues open to her, and that she will acquire her share of intellectual and moral development, happiness, and authority in her household...This would prove to be the most significant development in Egypt's history" (Amin 1995, 2). With his books *Tahrir Al-Mar'a* (Liberation of Women) and *Al- Mar'a Al-Jadida* (The New Woman), he called for the freedom of women, gender equality, and women's empowerment, supporting women's participation in the economic, social, and political affairs of the country (Elsadda and Abu-Ghazi, 38; Mariscotti 2008, 378; Sullivan 1986, 27; Botman 1999, 30). Amin, however, never challenged the Islamic framework in family matters, and the whole question of changing the Personal Status Laws was never addressed (Nelson 1996, 27). Besides, being himself a lawyer and judge, his pro-feminism discourse was considered dangerous by the most conservative religious leaders and by the lower classes (Badran 2009, 21). Because of his admiration for British customs and European progress, he was also accused of supporting colonialism and Western secularism. For Talaat Harb, the most prominent nationalist of the time, and his political opponent, the private sphere was the only suitable place for women, and the veil was a custom rendered compulsory by the *Shari'a* (Raccagni 1982, 99).

2.2 1919: Egyptian women between national activism and political segregation

At the turn of the nineteenth century, women contributed to the struggle against the armed forces of Napoleon Bonaparte through national and popular resistance; a similar courage was demonstrated during the Orabi revolution against Khedive Tewfik and the British invasion of the country in 1882 (Hussein 1953, 441). Toward the end of the century, women's involvement in the public sphere continued, mainly through philanthropic action. In early 1908, ruling-class women had begun to emerge from the isolation of their private life to work in charitable institutions, like *Mubarrat Mohamed Ali*, which assisted the population with the services of clinics, hospitals, and dispensaries (Guenena and Wassef 1999, 14). An early feminist discourse started to appear into the press in which women debated the "woman question" (*qadiyat al-mar'ah*), the role of women in the society. The new forum for the nascent Egyptian feminism was inaugurated by Hind Naufal with her journal *Al-Fatah* (The Young Woman) (Badran 2009, 20).

In 1919, the popular revolt against the British occupation started, and women strongly supported the nationalist movement fighting for independence. For the first time, ruling-class women joined the masses in nationalist militancy and political agitation, struggling not for a woman-based agenda, but rather for the same nationalist cause presented by men (Badran 2000; Sullivan 1986, 29). Young girls distributed leaflets; some guided the protests and met the leaders, others joined the streets with their families. Gender rules and divisions were completely suspended (Badran 1996, 74). Safeya Zaghloul, the wife of nationalist leader Saad Zaghloul, started to be called *Om El Masryeen*, the mother of the Egyptians, for her charismatic participation in the revolution (Baron 2005, 135). As Baron argues, "The Ladies'

Demonstration" of March 1919 soon became one of the most prominent icons of revolution (Ibid., 107). Women symbolized the true patriot, the revolution, and the nation (Ibid. 134).

On January 8, 1920, the first women's conference against British occupation was held in Cairo and attended by 500 women. The movement soon succeeded in establishing a relationship with nationalist leaders believing that a "modern state" should be preliminary to addressing the "woman question" (Fay 2003). Women's participation in the revolution did not itself produce feminism as ideology, but it gave women the political will to consolidate their claims on the nation (Badran 2009, 123). After the revolution, women appealed publicly to national leaders in articles, discussions, and meetings, asking for more rights in the welfare system and Personal Status Laws. However, they were soon excluded from those principles of liberty and individual rights that the revolution had promised to guarantee; they were denied the rights to vote and to hold political office. Women's support, which had served the nationalist cause during colonial occupation, was no longer seen by most men to be useful during the new period of independence (Badran 2009, 32). Once the militant struggle was over, the patriarchal milieu expected women to retreat to their homes. Besides, *Shari'a*-based family rules continued to represent the legacy of Islam in the judicial system in opposition to a complete secularization and Westernization of the country's laws (Haddad & Esposito 1998, xv; Abu-Odeh 2004, 1046; Mashhour 2005, 578; Bernard-Maugiron 2010, 3;6). Women, however, were increasingly leaving their homes and taking up new positions within society, becoming actively involved into a parallel isolated public sphere at the margins of masculine political life (Botman 1999, 28; Badran 1996). As Badran explains, this can be defined as the first wave of women's political feminism.

On March 16, 1923, Hoda Sha'rawi founded the Egyptian Feminist Union (EFU), *Al-Ittihad Al-Nisa'i Al-Misri,* the first feminist organization in Egypt and the Middle East, and was elected as its president, maintaining the position until 1947. In the same year, she led a delegation of women to the International Alliance of Women Summit in Rome, where upon her return she and her delegation took off their veils at the Cairo railway station in front of friends and supporters. This was an unprecedented gesture at the time and the starting point of women's battle against home segregation and social exclusion. In light of Sha'rawi's own experience with early marriage, one of the main priorities of the union was that of setting a legal minimum marriage age and amending family laws, such as men's easy access to divorce and polygamy. Other demands also concerned the independence of Egypt and Sudan, democratic principles to be included in the constitution, and the rights of women to education, political participation, and the vote (Abu Odeh 2004).

Egypt's feminist leaders joined diverse ideologies, but the movement was initially politically affiliated with the *Wafd* Party standing for the nationalist cause; the EFU was indeed in conjunction with the Wafdist Women's Central Committee (WWCC). Women, however, did not succeed in persuading male politicians to include women's rights in the secular legislation and policies of the state (Mariscotti 2008, 38). Although the WWCC and the EFU prepared and distributed *Les revendications des dames egyptienne* (The demands of Egyptian women), a sort of nationalist-feminist chart, women began to be rarely, if ever consulted (Badran 1996, 87). In a letter directed to the party, Sha'rawi stated that "women had simply been used by a group of men in the nationalist movement to mislead the civilized nations into believing in the maturity and advancement of the Egyptian nation and its ability to govern itself" (Ibid., 82). The patriarchal structure of the family also remained intact. New state officials were reluctant to irritate conservative groups in the first stages of national building, maintaining unaltered traditional social relations of the family. As Botman states, "the Egyptian liberalism merged with patriarchy to separate the public and the private arenas denying women the rights of citizenship" (Botman 1999, 25).

In 1924, the new Egyptian Constitution was ratified stating

that "all Egyptians are equal before the law. They enjoy equally civil and political rights and equally have public responsibilities without distinction of race, language, or religion." However, gender equality remained a mere speculation, as Article 1 for Law No.11 of 1923 restricted suffrage to males only (Badran 2009, 24; Guenena and Wassef 1999, 19). Since women could not aspire to achieve any imminent political success, the focus of the battle started to turn around the rights of women in the family. The union realized major achievements for Egyptian women, succeeding in increasing the age of boys and girls at marriage and extending the duration of women's custody of children in case of divorce (Abu Odeh 2004, 1100; Al-Ali 2002, 5; Elsadda and Abu-Ghazi, 101). Law No.25 of 1929, which the movement succeeded in pushing forward, gave women the right to ask for divorce, enabling judges to include several kinds of injury-causing factors, such as the protracted absence of the husband, his incurable defect, imprisonment, or failure to provide for the family's maintenance (Naveh 2001, 23; Bernard-Maugiron 2008; Al-Sharmani 2007, 6; Mashhour 2005, 575).

However, as Leila Ahmed puts it, the movement was influenced "by a Western affiliation and a Westernizing outlook and apparently by a valorization of Western ways as more advanced and more civilized than native ways" (Leila Ahmed 1993 in Fay 2003). While rural working women had access to the market, ruling-class women were secluded in their private harem, as work was still considered dishonorable for those women belonging to a certain class (Guenena and Wassef 1999, 13; Sullivan 1986, 25). Any of the issues related to the Personal Status Laws, like polygamy and men's right to divorce, may not have been as important to women of the lower class (Mariscotti 2008, 1). Lower-class men would have found it difficult to support more than one wife, while ruling-class women stood to lose more from divorce than did lower-class women, who were already engaged in some kinds of working activities (Ibid., 15). At that time, elite women were certainly suffering from a stronger form of patriarchal subordination, and their presence in the public arena served to challenge "patriarchal bargain," the sort of the male supremacy to which they were subjugated (Botman 1999, 110). Although at the beginning of their struggle Egyptian women also focused on a sort of pan-Arab and regional feminism, later on, as Mariscotti argues, the elitism of the movement and its affiliation with Western ideas of bourgeois feminism can be considered one of the main explanations for its failure. Feminist activism was limited to certain elitist sectors of society, and the sense was that those who were calling for certain rights were only secular women, not representatives of the majority of the female population. The cultural and social differences of the members of feminist groups also raised the question of their authenticity. The upper class had adopted elements of Western manners expressed in dress and in the use of the French language. Egyptian women did not benefit equally from secular feminist arguments, and efforts to help the poor mainly emphasized charitable work, not drastic change (Graham-Brown 1981). The EFU also introduced strict membership rules, making its access severely class-based and forbidding lower-class women from joining (Osman 2003, 36).

Therefore, some activists decided to leave the union, like Zainab al-Ghazali, who founded the Muslim Women's Society (MWS), a conservative women's political and religious movement, considered the first Islamic women's group in Egypt[16] (Karam 1998, 101). As Ahmed argues, Egyptian women have always been divided between those "eager to adopt European ways" and those who are "anxious to preserve the Islamic and national heritage against the onslaughts of the infidel West" (Ahmed 1993, 139 in Osman 2003, 33). While the EFU women found their feminist ideology compatible with Islam, however, as Badran explains, their overall ideological framework was definitely secular rather than religious. The EFU championed greater access for women to public roles and working positions, while the MWS mainly praised women's family duties and obligations (Badran 2009, 27).

2.3 From Nasser to Sadat: Women's rights amid Pan-Arabism and *infitah*

At the end of the '30s, the feminist movement was failing to address the needs of a broader constituency. Hence, women from the middle class started to change orientation, addressing political rights for women and the improvement of living conditions for poor urban and rural women (Badran 2009, 126). Doria Shafik became the second most important voice of the feminist movement in the mid-'50s. She established the association *Bint El Nil* (Daughters of the Nile), which later became a party demanding full constitutional rights for women (Nelson 1996, 154). By the end of the '50s, *Bint El Nil* was famous in the Middle East and among the Egyptian elite and popular urban quarters.

On February 19, 1951, almost 1,500 women from different political groups, headed by Shafik, organized a march on Parliament to demand their rights. During the demonstration, she declared, "my sisters, this is our first Parliament. It represents one half of the nation. I propose that we go there, strongly in knowledge of our right, and tell the deputies and senators that their assemblies are illegal as long as our representatives are excluded, that the Egyptian Parliament cannot be a true reflection of the entire nation until women are admitted" (Clark 1951). The women were told that their requests would be given serious thought, but the government remained silent. One of the Free Officers, Minister Ahmed Naguib, took a firm stand against the introduction of women's political rights as part of the government's electoral reform. A manifesto prepared by the *ulemas* and religious associations declared that "women's claim to political rights is an outrageous breach of religion. This movement is a serious threat to society's stability and solidarity and is insistent on the maintenance of the Islamic rule" (Nelson 1996, 183).

The Nasserist state instead became interested in obtaining the consensus of liberal factions of society, planning to give women more political rights in order to achieve this goal. Nasser adopted a socialist ideology and Pan-Arab doctrines in which women's integration was a crucial and fundamental element. On March 12, 1954, Shafik and eighteen other women went on a hunger strike in protest of the denial of women's political rights. They were promised that the matter would be considered this time by the new, socialist, revolutionary government. Nasser maintained the promise, and two years later, in 1956, the new Constitution guaranteed equality for all Egyptians, regardless of gender, as well as women's right to vote and to stand for elections in the Parliament (Sullivan 1986, 33; Al-Ali 2002, 7). This Constitution was actually the first Egyptian and Arab constitution to grant women the right to vote and run for office and to recognize women's citizenship. In 1957, for the first time, six women ran for elections and two of them won parliamentary seats (Hassan, Nasr and Morsy 2009, 41). Between 1956 and 1979, women started to assume political roles, enter Parliament and be appointed to cabinet posts. In 1959, the regime also introduced a new labor law that guaranteed new legal rights and special protection for working women and working mothers (Botman 1999, 59). In 1962, Nasser appointed Dr. Hekmat Abu Zeid, a woman, as minister of social affairs for the first time in modern history.

However, in contrast to a public domain, which was giving space to women's public roles, the Personal Status Laws were left to bear the marks of male privilege and gender disparity (Haddad & Esposito 1998, 89; Hatem 1986, 26). According to Al-Ali, even though Nasser's conversion to secularism and socialism was expected to guarantee social equality and new and more rights to all, the "resistance to Western cultural imperialism became equated with the preservation of existing gender relations, which consequently meant the perpetuation of patriarchal control" (Al-Ali 2002, 19). As Guenena and Wassef also put it, "women were perceived as the bearers and perpetuators of cultural values and social mores, which increased the resistance to any change in their status or the laws that govern their lives" (Guenena and Wassef 1999, 6). Conventional family life was preserved, and gender relations at home remained virtually unchallenged, despite formal political equality for women and their entitlement to public sector jobs. Feminism as independent public discourse was silenced as the state tried to determine citizens' rights within the framework of Arab socialism.

The EFU was dismantled in 1959, and al- Ghazali's Muslim Sisterhood was banned, as well as many other women-led organizations. Women's groups were absorbed into the only legal political organization, the Arab Socialist Union, and the nature of feminist activities remained limited to serving the party and the nation (Sullivan 1986, 23). Shafik, who condemned Nasser's brutal policies, started to be silenced by the military establishment, and her name was banned from any public action; she disappeared from public life and lived the rest of her life under arrest (Botman 1999, 67). Other feminists were either imprisoned or forced to close their political and social activities (Ibid.). A similar fate also happened to the Islamist al-Ghazali, who remained in prison for six years, suffering from torture and harassment.

Once in power, Sadat attempted to undermine the Nasserist and leftist frameworks in the country, seeking the support of Islamists and other middle-class political allies. But the alliance between the religious forces and the government had serious implications for women (Botman 1991, 79). Following the defeat of the 1967 war and the strong pressure of the Islamist movement, Sadat amended Article 2 of the Constitution in 1971, making the Islamic *Shari'a* one of the main sources of legislation, reflecting the government's willingness to embrace the Islamist discourse. The Constitution of 1971 contradicted the meaning of citizenship, stipulating that gender equality applies only when it does not interfere with the rules of *Shari'a* law. In 1980, the Constitution was amended once more, and *Shari'a* became the main source of legislation (Paonessa, 20; Botman 1991, 80). The state encouraged the new emphasis on religion accompanied by a shift from Pan-Arabism to *infitah* (open-door) capitalism (Badran 2009, 40). The contradictory pressures on women under Sadat were enormous. Because of the *infitah* and the limited success of privatization policies, the state no longer promoted the full employment of women, propagating instead an ideology that curtailed women's public roles, encouraging a retreat to their homes. Badran explains how, during the '70s, the popularity of the veil was perhaps connected with women's desire to work, participate in the public sphere, and to combat sexual harassment into the streets (Ibid., 42).

In another paradoxical move, the Parliament, through Law No.21 of 1979, instated a quota for women in Parliament, allocating thirty additional seats for women in the *Majlis al-Shaab* (The People's Assembly) (Hassan, Nasr and Morsy 2009, 42). Local government law was also changed to guarantee that 10 to 20 percent of the local council seats had to be reserved for women (Sulllivan 1986, 36). Thanks to the amendment, the presence of women in Parliament reached 9 percent in 1979. However, this first attempt to introduce a quota system for women in Parliament raised general discontent, and the law was considered unconstitutional for its alleged discrimination against men (Hassan, Nasr and Morsy 2009, 43).

In 1979, Sadat issued Decree-Law No.44, which gave women the right to unilateral divorce upon the second marriage of the husband without the first wife's consent. The law also stipulated the wife's right to remain in the conjugal home during the period of the custody of the children *(hadāna)*. In the following year, Egypt signed the UN Convention on the Elimination of All Forms of Discrimination Against Women (CEDAW). The Egyptian government ratified the articles that could have contradicted the *Shari'a* and Egyptian social norms, but it did so with reservations.[17] Sadat wanted to maintain Egypt's image abroad without handing over its political power to Islamists, who had a large following among the population (Sonneveld 2009, 34). The ratification of the CEDAW represented a significant move politically, indicating Egypt's willingness to adopt some of the norms and values recognized at the international level.

At the time of Sadat, a second wave of women's activism took shape. Among its leaders was Nawal al-Saadawi, who created the Arab Women Solidarity Association (AWSA). Saadawi, who became a popular icon of what Badran calls "sexual feminism," focused her struggle in fighting against the sexual oppression of women. Saadawi made public taboos that Egyptian society still considered unmentionable, provoking controversial and provocative debates with religious authorities.

Also, Jihan Sadat, the first lady, became a public personality for the defense of women's rights, pushing for the institutionalization of the National Commission for Women. Jihan played a key role in reforming Egypt's civil rights law, granting women several privileges concerning alimony and custody of children in case of divorce. Because of Jihan Sadat's ability as the president's wife to style herself the supreme advocate of women's causes in Egypt, the independent and radical feminism was not anymore tolerated in order to not reduce Jihan's prestige and subsequently to appease conservative Islamist forces.

However, the *"Jihan Laws"* were considered unconstitutional on procedural grounds and therefore illegitimate. For the most conservative MPs, Law No.44[18] was a clear violation of men's right to polygamy, and because polygamy is a right granted in the Islamic *Shari'a*, they believed it should not be considered evidence of injury to the first wife (Bernard-Maugiron, 2008; Naveh 2001, 29-30; Al-Sharmani 2007, 6; Hatem 1986, 37). Because of religious pressures and a long campaign against it, Law No.44 was replaced by Law No.100 of 1985, which placed restrictions on previous reforms (Mashhour 2005, 578; Naveh 2001, 30; Esposito 2001, 62). The High Constitutional Court's judgment was considered "a success for Islamists and a blow to reformers" (Moussa, 15). This law hindered efforts toward women's rights, requesting the proof of physical or moral harm derived from a polygamous marriage, putting upon women the burden of bringing witnesses in order to provide evidence of harm (Naveh 2001, 31; Bernard-Maugiron 2010, 6). Despite Jihan Sadat's personal struggle for a better welfare system in the country and gender equality, she was identified with Western elitism, and her egotism started to disturb the average Egyptian. For the conservative sections of society, Mrs. Sadat's interference in the Personal Status Laws was perceived as the ultimate proof of a conspiracy against *Shari'a*. Hence, because of her interest in women's issues, the feminist movement started to be identified with the regime and women's problems passed on the second level, even though the two were fundamentally separated (Botman 1991, 81). When the regime lost the support of the people, the women's movement suffered as a result. Besides, with the end of Sadat's era, women still lacked independent and strong organizations and there was still not a general state program to promote women's rights (Al-Ali 74, 2000).

2.4 Women's rights during Mubarak's time
At the time of Mubarak, political debate remained anchored on the issue of granting women more and new rights. Mubarak found himself trapped into the same challenge that faced Sadat. The regime wanted to appear reformist and progressive towards women's issues but did so while trying to relegate women to the sidelines of the political mainstream (Botman 1999, 92). Once in power, the system of legislative quota introduced by Sadat was at first reversed by Mubarak in order to placate Islamists (who had entered Parliament in 1987) and disengage from the controversial feminist policies associated with Sadat and his wife (Ibid., 91). However, the Egyptian government, in the light of the commitments taken at international

level[19] and the political aspiration of finding an ally in the West, made incredible efforts toward the achievement of women's equality under the law, launching in 2000 a new Personal Status Law.[20] The decision was made on the basis of different needs, among them: "strengthening state institutions, creating equality and justice for all citizens, making claims to religious and cultural legitimacy, improving the status of Egypt within the international community, and securing the support of international organizations" (Al Sharmani, 2007). The new law introduced two significant articles for women. Article 17 granted women in unregistered marriages (*urfi*) the right to file for divorce, while Article 20 gave women the right to file for a no-fault divorce named *khul'*. Contrary to fault-based divorce, the *khul'* was seen as a revolutionary achievement, granting women irrevocable judicial separation without a need to justify their reasons, whether or not the husband agrees, and maintaining the financial obligations he has for the children[21] (Arabi 2001, 171; Bernard-Maugiron 2010, 22; Zantout 2006). However, the *khul'* law was received by Egyptian society with diverse opinions, generating an animated debate on different fronts. As with Law No.44 of 1979, attempt at reform quickly became politicized, bringing protest and dissent. *Khul'* would turn upside down a marriage system that depends both legally and socially on the maintenance-obedience relation. Family laws place the protection of the family unit above individual rights within the family, giving men privileges to assume the role of sole provider. A power game was once again played out through control over women's rights, using religion as an alibi. In spite of objections from the most conservative MPs and many religious scholars, Grand Sheikh of *Al-Azhar* Sayyid Tantawi and the Islamic Research Academy approved the *khul`* as conforming to the *Shari'a* (Arabi 2001, 172; Mashhour 2005, 583; Moussa 2006, 18; Tucker 2008, 129). With this move, Egypt also demonstrated an ability to respect some of its international obligations to equality in family relations without displacing religious laws altogether (Moussa, 2). Hence, the *khul'* reform is part of what Welchman calls a third phase of Muslim Personal Status Law transformation in the Arab world in which, due to "changed global, regional and national circumstances in Arab states... amendments to Muslim family law demonstrate an intense political contingency reflecting national and international pressures and dynamics" (Welchman 2007, 42-3 in Sonneveld 2009, 2).

Other changes that have been made pertaining to women in recent years during the control of the National Democratic Party (NDP) also consisted of lifting the long-standing restriction on female judges in the Supreme Judicial Council, amending the nationality law and the Child Law which includes a condemnation of the practice of the FGM, and increasing the minimum marriage age for women to eighteen. Another has been the readoption of the women's parliamentary quota, which will be examined further in this study. Most of these changes have been achieved, thanks to significant campaigns that women's groups and NGOs have carried out throughout the years. For years, different women's groups have produced several reports about the need to introduce these decrees. However, the NDP has long been reluctant to introduce such amendments until Suzanne Mubarak, through her position at the National Council of Women (NCW), started to exert a lot of effort in this regard to support women's cause. As Shoukry, former member of the NDP women's committee, reported, "appointing women as judges was the result of efforts by the first lady ... and the NDP as a whole had nothing to do it" (Dawood 2010, 75). According to Dawood, this clearly shows how the NDP did not have any concrete decision-making power for matters related to women's rights, and changing laws has been done at the discretion of the president and the first lady (Ibid., 110). Also for this reason, the role of the National Council for Women (NCW) and its relation with women's groups has been conflicting and antagonistic on several occasions during Mubarak's regime. Some women's groups have repeatedly accused the national council of taking credit for some of the successes achieved by the NGOs. As Nawla Darwish, president of the New Woman Foundation (NWF), argued, "the extensive coverage by the government owned media of this Council's [NCW] marvelous achievements under the leadership of Egypt's first lady, as well as this Council's message, which is devoid of any truly empowering discourse to Egyptian women ... has backfired among Egyptian laymen and women and has led to an increase in opposition for women's rights, not to mention making fun of women's rights" (Darwish and Shukrala 2006, 16 in Dawood 2010, 130). On more than one occasion, the NCW has been also accused of having used the donors' funds for ambiguous activities. It seems that the NCW has tried to co-opt women's NGOs, using them as vehicles for implementing its vision, policies, and activities (Ibid., 138). As Hoda Badran, chairperson of the Alliance for Arab Women (AAW) reiterated during our interview:

"The establishment of the NCW was a good initiative. The presidential decree, which established the NCW and described its functions, was good indeed. For two or three years it went well. But then, the secretary-general changed, and the country changed. Suzanne Mubarak also changed, and the system was escalating the corruption. That council, instead of serving women's causes, started to serve itself, getting more staff, building its ego. Mrs. Suzanne Mubarak was on the news every day. People started to get annoyed by her. The council started to compete with the NGOs instead of backing the NGOs; the council started to get donors' money and to compete with the NGO for funds. When we did good things, they took the credit." [22]
And also for Imen Bibars, chair of the Association for Development and Enhancement of Women (ADEW):

"We were not enemies with the government, but we were not friends. We were pragmatic. Sometimes we had to use the government to improve women's lives. We were attacking the policies of the government, its program, but not the government itself. We were never confrontational. But we had many frustrations. The system was corrupted. The NCW had identity crises. When it was created, I thought that it was a good idea to have an organism representing women issues. The problem is that it became a political apparatus, and it started to compete with the NGOs. And it took the credit for everything the NGOs were pushing for. And they took also money and credit from us. Ms. Mubarak was in the newspaper every day." [23]

For Kandiyoti, indeed the creation of the NCW can be described as a sort of "gender conditionality," a soft option for Arab regimes to take rather than truly adopting agendas in favor of women's rights. Progress on women's rights issues could thus be deployed as an apparent democratic façade (Kandiyoti 2011). Egypt seems to support women's rights when it is convenient, and women's issues have often been used as a bargaining tool in the international arena.

This outward pro-women's rights agenda can also be uncovered when looking at the political participation of women. In 2009, the People's Assembly Law No.38 of 1972 was amended to provide a quota of sixty-four seats for women. Nevertheless, under Mubarak, the political representation of women in Parliament had remained almost insignificant: in 2000, women held only eleven seats (2.49 percent) (Mustafa, Shukor and Rabi' 2005, 10). Although the NDP was in power for more than three decades, the number of women in decision-making positions remains extremely limited. Besides, although the quota system did increase women's representation in the Parliament, it also ensured further power and more seats to the NDP, boosting general opposition to the introduction of this law. In the course of the last century, limited female political representation has not only been confined to the legislature or participation in general elections, but it has also been extended to women's presence in political life in general. The contribution of Egyptian women to the activity of political parties has been extremely weak, if not absent altogether (Ibid, 24). The programs of all Egyptian political parties, despite their different ideologies, advocated the need for a suitable environment to help women exercise their rights and duties. However, in reality, political parties continue to work against such proposals. In the *Wafd* party, out of sixty decision-makers, there were only three women before the revolution. For Korashi, a member of the *Wafd* women's committee, male members of the *Wafd*, as in any other party, consider women's rights dangerous, and that is why most of the women's committees within parties are largely inactive (Dawood 2010, 78). Farida Naqash, one of the founding members of the *Tagammu'* party, reports that:

"In the Parliamentary elections of 2005, the Tagammu' party was the only party—other than the NDP—that nominated two women, although they both lost the elections. Also, in 2010, the percentage of women candidates from the Tagammu' was 12 percent. The Tagammu' also has consisted in a progressive women's union, which is a semi-independent organization whose leaders are members of the higher party council. The party has used the quota system since its establishment, though the number of women in the party is still low." [24]

Thus, it can be questioned to what extent political parties have truly taken up the issue of political participation of women, whether inside the party or outside through candidacy on electoral lists. It is obvious that women's political participation has always lagged behind the level of rights recognized in the Constitution and the laws regarding women. During the time of the three presidents, women's political participation did not meet the nationalistic aspirations of the struggle for the independence in 1919 (Mustafa, Shukor and Rabi' 2005, 24). Instead, for more than a century, women's rights have constantly been shaped and reshaped according to internal and external dynamics that have seen the country divided between a domestic reformist push for women's emancipation, a lasting conservatism, and an external need to please the West and its international institutions (Haddad & Esposito 1998, 3).

Besides, if for some scholars, women's rights have mainly been hampered by conservative religious interpretations; for others, like Al-Ali, "the lack of existing democratic models and experiences in democratic political structures posed the most enormous challenge to women's rights activists" (El-Mahdi 2010, 384).

2.5 Sub-conclusion

Egypt is similar to the cases of Algeria, Morocco, and Iran, where women's rights have been manipulated by the state, reflecting the economic and political interests of the regime in power. As Botman argues, "throughout very different political regimes prevailing gender ideologies served state power, reinforced religious doctrine, and strengthened the patriarchal paradigm" (Botman 1999, 111). Gender issues were used by the state and its allies to achieve ideological and political victories both nationally and internationally (Ibid.). A substratum of gender inequality has always remained intact, challenging neither patriarchal relations nor the state's own ambiguities and contradictory moves (Badran 2009, 47).While during the liberal era, women's participation in the national struggle was welcomed, once the state consolidated its authority, it did not incorporate women into the rank of citizens. Despite the efforts of the early feminist movement in Egypt, the advancement of women's rights did not come. As Nawal El Saadawi said in this regard, "The movement was not representative of the overwhelming majority of toiling women, and its leadership ended, just as the political leadership did, by seeking accommodations with the British, the palace and the reactionary forces in the country. The women's movement ... kept away from an active involvement in the national and political life of the country, and limited its activities to charitable and social welfare work" (Baker 1998, 274). Indeed, in Egypt, women's rights have not been included into the secular legislation and policies of the state, and women began to be rarely, if ever, politically consulted (Mariscotti 2008, 38; Badran 1996, 87).

Despite the fact that few civil and political rights were guaranteed to women under the three presidents, their status clearly remained subordinated in family matters. Family has been always represented the area in which the state has allowed patriarchal control, using women's rights as a bargaining chip to contain Islamists' requests.

The state has clearly used the "woman question" for its own interests, never challenging the patriarchal structure of the society and a rising conservative social discourse. Furthermore, feminist groups have failed to create strong and enduring constituencies with different political voices of the country and to fuse in one unified political and ideological agenda. Besides, as the last part of the chapter has shown, the ambiguous relations of women's groups with the regime and in a special way, their "prima donnas," Jihan Sadat and Suzanne Mubarak, made the society inevitably uninterested in the "woman question." When the regime lost the support of the people, the women's movement suffered the consequences.

CHAPTER III

WOMEN AMIDST POLITICAL ACTIVISM, AND THE TRANS-FORMATIONS OF POST-MUBARAK EGYPT

This chapter opens with a short analysis of the main factors that ignited the popular rebellion that lead to the revolution of January 25. This chronological background analysis is important to link the past with the present and to investigate the current events. The chapter continues with a description of the revolution itself, which I personally witnessed in Tahrir Square, by describing one of the components that, more than others, has attracted the attention politicians worldwide: the strong presence of women. Although the previous chapter has underlined that women's roles in independence struggles are not new phenomena, the recent revolution taking place in Egypt and the dynamism through which women have launched and participated in street protests without being marginalized and/or harassed took many Western observers by surprise. But the main meaningful aspect learned from the previous chapter in regard to the transitional post-revolution periods has been the general unaltered—if not, regressive—aftermath that transitional gender politics has brought to women's rights. Thus, this chapter first seeks to analyze if and how, once the initial revolutionary euphoria has settled down, the post-Mubarak state will differentiate its approach by studying the new consequences for the social and political rights of women. This will be done by reporting the governmental policies toward women's political inclusion and social attitudes about women's political roles in transition. Second, the chapter will look at the various forms of women's political participation and civil activism by analyzing the actions of old and new women's groups and NGOs, how they have adjusted their demands, their current directions, and which successes and/ or problems they are currently facing. Third, the chapter will conclude by reporting the current escalating role of political Islam and the visions and attitudes adopted by the main groups in regard to the advancement of women's rights in Egypt.

So the question becomes, as we turn to a transitioning Egypt: what will happen to women's political and public roles in a country like Egypt, which is planning to become a real democracy? How is the transition including women's demands for political and social equality? Is women's activism increasing and, if so, how do women's groups and NGOs respond, specifically toward new democratic openings and political possibilities? How is political Islam interfering within the newly reformulated "woman question"?

This chapter draws on numerous "elite interviews" with feminists or women's rights advocates[23], political activists or media experts, members of the Muslim Brotherhood, specialists in Islamic law, and academics. I chose to interview people who are active in society and concerned with the question of women's public roles. I was also eager to orient myself toward what normal people thought in order to make broader comparisons. This will be analyzed in the following chapter.

3.1 The awakening of Arab dignity: the case of Egypt, triggers, and causes

The Middle Eastern revolutions are absolute new phenomena in recent world history. In Tunisia, Egypt, Libya, Syria, and Yemen, the time has come to call for the end of a regional system based on authoritarianism, corruption, nepotism, and favoritism; the time has come to introduce a "moral hygiene," a general rejection of the illegitimacy of Arab despots and their servants. The awakening of Arab dignity started in Tunisia. Mohammed Bouazizi, a twenty-six-year-old street vendor from the impoverished town of Sidi Bouzid, ignited the revolt by setting himself ablaze to protest police brutality, unemployment, and poverty. Popular protests immediately started in the area and continued until January 14, the day on which President Ben Ali and his family were forced to leave on an airplane to Saudi Arabia. Between the end of 2010 and the beginning of 2011, the Tunisians brought down one of the most corrupt and stable regimes in the Middle East, becoming an inspiring force for the rest of the region pushing populations to have higher expectations of change (Noor 2011).

For a long time, Egyptian society had been excluded from any political democratic process, and the risks of any sort of political activism had been too high for the normal Egyptian to engage in it; the attitude had been that of passive compliance and acceptance of scarce political alternatives (Kamrava 2005, 343). Following the effects of the Nasserism and Sadatism, under the regime of Mubarak, political groups continued to be banned, with the Muslim Brotherhood movement and militant communists working underground. In early 2005, an engineer and political militant, Saad Bahaar, entered into contact with a group of three activists expatriated to England, deciding together to create the Academy of Change, defined as a "window for Egypt's activists into civil disobedience movements outside the Arab world" (Awad and Dixon 2011). Thanks to the activities of academics who started training members of the *Kefaya* movement[25] on civil rebellion, a revolt was launched in December 2006 by more than 20,000 textile workers from the Nile Delta city of Mahalla El Kobra, staging a six-day strike. Following this event, some former members of *Kefaya* formed the "April 6 group," using the Internet to gather supporters and adopting the civil disobedience techniques of the Serbian movement *Otpor* (Amnesty International 2011, 16). In 2009, demonstrations calling for political and economic reforms increased, mainly led by *Kefaya*, the April 6 Youth Movement, and the Muslim Brothers. The April 6 Youth Movement, initiated by Ahmed Maher and Ahmed Salah in spring 2008, was quickly joined by hundreds of youth with strong democratic beliefs, a vision, and careful coordination on the ground. Together with other political forces, the group called for a general strike on January 25 to protest the country's economic crisis and the deteriorating living conditions of the Egyptian population. The hundreds of thousands of youth across Egypt who marched, chanted, and demonstrated were young men and women with university degrees, living constrained by the lack of employment, opportunities, and justice.

The Egyptian revolution, like many other uprisings in the region, is a result of a complex range of social, economic, political, and geo-political factors. The first factor was the democratic deficit, due to an authoritarian rule that has curtailed freedom and people's rights for decades. Under the "*mukhaberat* state," most people participated in presidential elections knowing fully well that the political outcome was predetermined. State authoritarianism was characterized by the absence of strong, autonomous political institutions and groupings able to challenge the ruler's personal monopoly on power (Kassem 2004, 341). Also, the freedom deficit and the legal restrictions placed on civil society organizations and political groups have stymied political openness and democracy, leading to a larger prominence of the most conservative religious organizations. The economic and demographic conditions, with high rates of unemployment and poverty, have especially plagued Egypt. In 2009, around 32 million of Egypt's 80 million people were living on or near the poverty line of $2 a day, and the average per-capita income in the country was just $6,200 (Arab Human Development Report 2009, 11). For almost 25 years, the minimum wage has not risen for the majority of the population, contrary to the high wages of a group of major employers, both foreign and national. The ruling elite and President Mubarak's family and friends continued to be the only beneficiaries of the open economy, accumulating millions of dollars in private banks all around the world. The regime's economic policies, free market, and privatization led to a poverty rate of more than 40 percent among the Egyptian population (El-Nakash 2011, 1). In addition, the interference of the International Monetary Fund made the overall picture look even worse in early 1987, when it became clear that Egypt was not able to repay its foreign debt. In 1991, Egypt signed the stabilization and structural adjustment agreement with the fund, which pushed for privatization, derogation, and devaluation as conditioned by the World Bank, the IMF, and WTO (Amin 2011, 17). Nevertheless, the Egyptian economy has been growing fast from 2006 to 2008, at 7 percent a year, continuing to increase

by 6 percent even during the global crisis (Bryjak 2011). Egypt's GDP grew approximately 5 percent in 2010, and one-fifth of Egyptians believed economic conditions were getting better (Abu Dhabi Gallup Center). As political observer and commentator Fareed Zakaria argues, the Arab case can be explained by referring to Tocqueville's theory of "rising expectations" (RRE) (Parks 2011). The theory, looking at the example of the French revolution and other revolts, explains that uprisings are often initiated by those classes that see their economic and social status improving but not fast enough. "Their 'expectations' are rising faster than their ability to realize these expectations and a frustration 'gap' emerges between what people have and their belief about what they should have—what they rightfully deserve" (Bryjak 2011). Indeed, Egyptian economic growth only reached a small group of people while others encountered frustration, stimulated by economic difficulties such as high unemployment, poor quality of education, high costs of housing, and limitations to citizenship.

Even though it is fundamental to recognize that chants and slogans during the Arab revolutions have been empty of anti-U.S. and anti-Israel rhetoric, it is unquestionable that the array of Arab leaders in protection of U.S.-Israeli interests is also a definitive cause of anger among Arab populations. The land of Palestine, for more than 50 years, has been the core of regional political concerns. The recent war in Gaza, the massacre of its population, and Mubarak's role in maintaining Gaza obstructed, increased the resentment of Egyptians toward the regime's connivance with Israel (Kings and Cabbages 2011). The subjugation of Egypt to Israel and the U.S. goes back to the time of President Nixon, when to liberate Sinai from Israeli occupation, Egypt was requested to rearm itself with American weaponry in order to open the Egyptian economy to a flux of Western capital (Amin 2011, 14). In 1979, the Egypt-Israel peace treaty, signed by Sadat and Israeli Prime Minister Menachem Begin, made Egypt the first Arab country to officially recognize the state of Israel. As part of the agreement, the U.S. began substantial levels of economic aid, granting $1.1 billion as result of the peace agreement and $1.5 billion in military assistance. Throughout the 1980s and 1990s, the U.S. granted Egypt economic and military aid of $2.2 billion annually (Rutherford 2008, 5; Yuval). Finally, the U.S. wars in Iraq and Afghanistan and the war on terror, with the subsequent international detestation for the Islamic religion and Arabs in general, has been definitely another cause of frustration for foreign policies adopted by Western countries and for their alliances with corrupt Arab regimes.

3.2 A modern *thawra*: the making of a revolution

Also in the Egyptian case, the spark that caused the revolt to break out has been analogous to the Tunisian case of Mohammed Bouazizi. One year ago, anger started to arouse among Egypt's youth after police killed a young man, Khaled Saeed, in June 2010. Wael Ghonim, an activist and head of marketing for the Middle East and North Africa at Google, created a webpage on Facebook called *"Kolena Khaled Saeed"* (We're All Khaled Saeed), calling for ending police brutality and the Emergency Law. In late 2010, the Khaled Saeed page on Facebook invited the entire population to the same nationwide march. However, other significant events occurred in Egypt prior to the revolution that increased frustration and pressure among Egyptians. The first is the return in Egypt of Mohamed ElBaradei, former director general of the International Atomic Energy Agency (IAEA), who had been opposing Mubarak's regime for the last couple of years. The second event forged parliamentary elections in 2010, which was considered among the most disgraceful elections in Egypt's history. Only 28 percent of Egyptians said that they trusted the parliamentary elections and their results in 2005 and 2010 (Abu Dhabi Gallup Center 2011). The elections of 2010 were thoroughly corrupt and strengthened popular resentment toward Mubarak. The Muslim Brotherhood's representation in Parliament dropped from eighty-eight to zero (Amnesty International 2011, 17).

Hence, as Esraa Abdel Fatteh, a member of the April 6 Youth Movement, explained during a conference I attended in April organized by Karama, a woman's NGO:

"The revolution did not come overnight, there was a long preparation. All these events accumulated and culminated into the explosion of the population. As for January 25, the goals of the march were mainly three: (1) to dismiss the Ministry of Interior, and the dissolution of Parliament; (2) social demands, like minimum wages;

(3) the end of the Emergency Law."[26]

Afef El Saeed, radical feminist and executive director of the *Heya* Foundation for Women, explained that she had been preparing for the revolt one month before the events oc- curred, posting on the page of "We're All Khaled Saeed" and organizing for the demonstration with members of the *Kefaya* movement.[27] But as Esraa Abdel Fatteh emphasized, no one was expecting that an event of this magnitude might happen; the revolution took the world by surprise. The Egyptian Revolu- tion, inspired by the Tunisian uprising, started as a youth-led revolution on January 25, 2011. Someone even called this revo- lution "the Facebook revolution" made by the Facebook gener- ation (Smith 2011). It is undeniable that the social media have played a key role in giving the youth an independent means of communication, propaganda, and cyber-political activism. The eighteen days of protests took place in a country that was considered to have an anesthetized political life and a highly sophisticated repressive apparatus consisting of more than two million members, ensuring a long legacy of authoritarian con- tinuity.

There are two significant aspects about the nature of this upris- ing; the leaderlessness of the movement and the significant role of youth. The quasi-absence of leadership or a clear ideological agenda facilitated the participation of different social sectors that usually abstained from politics under the old regime. Moreover, the significant role youth played through using mod- ern means of communications contributed to the mobilization of people who were regarded as "apolitical," and this made it harder for the old regime to control the technological trends. While youth were the driving force in the preparation phase and in the early days, the revolution quickly became national in every sense: during the days of the revolution, an increasingly diverse demographic mix in demonstrations was witnessed. People from all age groups, social classes, men and women, Mus- lims and Christians, urban people and peasants, and members of the upper- and lower-middle classes came out in large numbers with a determination rarely seen before. As Dalia Ziada, blogger, activist, and founder of the American Islamic Congress in Egypt, explained during our interview:

"I noticed immediately that this revolt was something bigger. I didn't see only the usual faces I was used to seeing during demonstrations. This was a real popular uprising. I understood that it was really happening."[28]

Activists of the April 6 Youth Movement and the Muslim Brotherhood, which joined the protests few days later, formed the strongest lines of opposition, also ensuring security in *Tahrir* Square during the eighteen days of the uprising. The number of protesters increased, and the main slogans became "Down with Mubarak" and "The people want to overthrow the regime." They also became the main slogans of the popular uprisings in Yemen, Libya, and Syria (El-Nakash 2011, 3). Even though, as I just said, the revolution was considered leaderless, diverse forces participated in the demonstrations. Liberal voices guided by Mohamed ElBaradei, as well the religious forces of the Muslim Brotherhood, all entered into the playing field for the demonstrations. Despite the shutting down of communication technologies, including Internet and mobile phones, the protests continued across several cities in the following days, and hundreds of protesters were arrested. The protests became stronger on January 28, when people, women and men, came out calling for "Bread, freedom, and social justice," showing solidarity and unity. On this "Day of Anger," protesters encountered police brutality in which various sorts of weapons were used to control mass protests. Mubarak and his followers tried to control the situation through a series of speeches, addressing the people, but they came very slow compared to the momentum of the protests. At the same time, President Mubarak appointed Omar Suleiman as vice president and Ahmed Shafik as prime minister. Both these figures being military men from Mubarak's entourage—Suleiman being the chief of the

Egyptian Intelligence Service and Shafik being the former commander of the Air Force—their names were promptly refused. On February 1, Mubarak also announced that he was not going to seek another term in office and that his son Gamal would no longer be standing for election as president. On February 2, thugs and pro-Mubarak groups attacked the protestors in *Tahrir* Square on a day that came to be known as "The Battle of the Camel," killing hundreds of civilians. Finally, on February 11, after eighteen days of protests, Omar Suleiman, in a press release circulated at 6 p.m., announced the resignation of Hosni Mubarak as president of Egypt, allocating power to the Supreme Council of the Armed Forces (SCAF) (Amin 2011, 12).

3.3 Taking to the streets: 2011 like 1919

"We want to go down to Tahrir Square on January 25. If we still have honor and want to live in dignity on this land, we have to go down on January 25. We'll go down and demand our rights, our fundamental rights. . . . Your presence with us will make a difference, a big difference!"
Asmae Mahfouz (Badran 2011).

Women in the revolutions of 1919 and 2011 (Source: Google)

The Egyptian revolution saw an incredible and unprecedented participation of women among the ranks of its activists. One of the most notorious faces of this revolution is indeed that of a young lady, Asmae Mahfouz, a member of the April 6 Youth Movement who launched a video call in January in which she urged "all young men and women" to join the demonstration against the regime. In her video, she called on Egyptians to demand their rights and to create the political change that they wish to see (Mekay 2011). One of the protest organizers was also a woman, the political militant Esraa Abdel Fattah, whose fifteen-day detention in 2008 for her activism made her a symbol of resistance. It had been a long time since Egypt witnessed so many women together acting in the public sphere and demanding their rights. This image went back in time to 1919, when Safeya Zaghloul led the revolt in Tahrir Square. Since the beginning of the demonstrations, women and girls from all sectors of society and different areas in Egypt participated in the protests, standing in the front lines, protecting others and insisting on their demands to have a better future for Egypt. During the eighteen days of the revolution, women played several roles socially and politically. Some women formed clinics in the square and inside *Omar Makram* mosque, helping to nurse the wounded; in addition, they cleaned the square and distributed food and water to those who had a sit-in there. At its height, unconfirmed statistics state that roughly one-quarter of the million protesters who poured into the square each day were women. As Fatema Khafagy, activist, gender expert, and board member of the Alliance for Arab Women (AAW), told me:

"There were hundreds of women involved in organizing supplies, medications, banners, marches, international contacts, and general mobilization for this revolution. Women have been distributing blankets, but they have been also protecting their streets day and night from acts of vandalism." [29]

Indeed, some women insisted on spending nights in the square, with their families and friends or even alone, confident in their responsibility to ensure the success of the revolution. Veiled and unveiled women shouted, fought, and slept in the streets alongside men, upending traditional expectations of their behavior. Others held signs with powerful messages that called for bringing down the regime and former president Mubarak. Also, for Ayyash Abdel Rahman, a liberal Islamist and ex-member of the Muslim Brotherhood:

"Some of our sisters slept in the square, although many others did not participate in the demonstrations because of family restrictions. Women's political participation is not only a good thing, it is necessary." [30]

Women are also part of the long list of those injured by security forces or "thugs," like Moheer Khalil Zaki, from Boolaq El Dakroor in Giza, who was shouted when she was witnessing to the killing of a man from the window of her home (Amnesty International 2011, 23). Or Sally Zahran, killed during the Friday of Anger by thugs who beat her with a bludgeon. Thus, as Wolf puts it, "women in Egypt didn't just 'join' the protests, but they were a leading force behind the Cultural Revolution that made the protests inevitable" (Wolf 2011). Wolf's words are confirmed by Dalia Ziada, who says that:

"Women have played a magnificent role in the revolution. It was the first time to see women so powerful. I saw very old women standing in front of policemen and asking them, 'Why are you doing this to your brothers?' Women were also inspiring people, especially men. If someone wanted to leave the battle, some other people would say, 'Are you going and women are staying'?"

Also, for Dr. Hamdy El Hennawi, a gender expert:

"Women's participation has been a key element for the success of the revolution. I went through this image several times, of men defending women when there was an attack from the thugs; men would be ashamed to run away and to not defend women."[31]

Women were the backbone of this movement; without them, this movement would not have lasted that long. This is because when women did not stay at home, avoiding being in danger as they always did, they equalized themselves with men, and this gave more motivation for everyone to hold on and stay together. Afef El Saeed also stressed on the complementary nature of the women's movement. She said that she expected to see secular women activists in the demonstrations but was impressed to see many ordinary women with such strong patriotic and civil ideas. These groups, she said, complemented each other in their social backgrounds and requests, some asking for a political turnover while others asked for economic progress. The square also made women feel secure, introducing gender equality between men and women and showing respect and acceptance. As Hania Sholkamy, an activist and AUC assistant professor says, recalling Margot Badran in the revolution of 1919, "the revolt that has brought the end of Mubarak's regime has been absolutely gender neutral; Tahrir Square became for eighteen days the microcosm of the perfect Egyptian society" (Sholkamy 2011). Also, Dina Wahba, a young female activist adds:

"What changed me during the revolution was "acceptance". I felt accepted and safe. We were invited by men to chant with them and we never felt we were different." [32]

It is noteworthy indeed that except for the case of the assault of South African journalist Lara Logan, during the eighteen days of the revolution, not a single case of harassment was reported.[33]

3.4 Women & politics in the transition: missing the gains of the revolution

Like the revolution of 1919, women's participation in the national movement of January 25 was welcomed, and it became a social obligation to support the liberation efforts. However, in the initial phase of the transitional period, women began to be excluded from the highest levels of decision making for the reform processes currently underway. Like in 1919, women defended the country in a time of crisis, but in "normal" times, men are to command the public sphere (Badran 135, 1993).

As the comparative analysis proposed in the second chapter suggests, this seems to be a typical trend for post-revolutionary and transitional countries. As Waylen explains, "once the transition has begun and political parties have reconstituted and resumed their activities, the focus tends to shift away from women's organizations and social movements in general and toward more conventional forms of institutional politics, particularly when the opening is controlled by the military" (Waylen 1994, 339). Once competitive politics start to re-establish activities thanks to the new political opening, it is clear that for the weakest groups, participation in national liberations does not necessarily guarantee an important role in the outcome. Women's groups are left with the choice that has been summed up as the dilemma of "autonomy" versus "integration" (Ibid.).

In Egypt, it is evident that the current political changes have had so far negative implications for women. Immediately after the end of the revolt, women started to be excluded from the consultations related to the constitutional process. Egypt's constitution has been suspended since February 14, three days after Hosni Mubarak left office. The reformed constitution will temporarily guide the nation until the final drafting of the new constitution, presumably in mid-2012 following the three rounds of parliamentary elections. First presented on February 26, the amendments were drafted by a committee, headed by Tarek El Beshri, appointed by the supreme military council. El Beshri is a respected judge who criticized former president Hosni Mubarak and is regarded as moderate in his views. But he has been associated with Al-Wasat, an offshoot of the Brotherhood (Spencer 2011). The civil group committee, which prepared recommendations for the amendments, was comprised of ten members and called by women activists the "Council of Wise Men," as it did not include a single woman, although many reputable female Egyptian lawyers could have easily served, such as Tahani El Gebali, Egypt's first female judge, appointed to the Constitutional Court in 2003 (Power 2011). The proposed constitutional changes addressed Articles 75, 76, 88, 93, 139, 148, and 189. A newly formed coalition of women's NGOs called "The Egyptian Coalition for Civic Education and Women's Participation" prepared a petition addressing the ruling army council and lamenting the amendment of Article 75, calling for a rewording of what follows:

"Egypt's President is born to two Egyptian parents and cannot be married to a non-Egyptian woman. Neither he nor his parents shall have another nationality except the Egyptian one. He shall practice his own civil and political rights."

According to the Egyptian Center for Women Rights (ECWR), which is leading the newborn coalition, Article 75 limits the presidency to men only, as the phrase ألا يكون متزوجاً من غير مصري —"cannot be married to a non-Egyptian woman"—is a statement limited to the spouse of a man. The ECWR suggested instead that the text should read "shall not be married to a non-Egyptian." When women NGOs protested, those responsible argued that Arabic allows masculine nouns to include women. But Nehad Abol Komsan, chair of the ECWR and a lawyer expert in Islamic *Shari'a*, explained how the Arabic language does not have a noun as a reference to both men and women.

Subsequently, a referendum was held on March 19 on these amendments, which passed (approximately 77 percent were in favor, while 23 percent opposed the changes). The voter turnout marked the highest in Egypt's modern history, with approximately 41 percent (18 million) out of 45 million eligible voters. However, there was much debate about the constitutional referendum, which had a direct relation to political parties' formation. Most of the people who opposed the amendments argued that holding parliamentary elections too soon will only favor of the well-organized Muslim Brotherhood and the members of Mubarak's former National Democratic Party.[34] Thus, the Parliament will not represent the majority of Egyptians, who were apolitical for the past thirty years and who were the real drivers of change in the revolution.

Different groups have been working to create new political parties, promote candidates, and increase turnout among their supporters. However, very few parties pushed for women's issues within their platforms. One example is that of the Free Egyptian Party, launched by business tycoon Naguib Sawiris, which announced the inclusion of a women's program within its agenda. However, it is not yet clear how this agenda will be pushed forward. The Egyptian Social Democratic Party, a liberal and secular party, seems to be more concretely inclusive as it immediately formed a women's committee. Women can be also found on the party council, which is planning to field candidates. The women's commission of the Popular Socialist Coalition Party held workshops to brainstorm recommendations for Egyptian women during the transition period and to further develop a program for the empowerment of women (Abuelgar 2011). Fatma Khafagy, a member of the party says:

"Some parties are integrating women's demands. The Social Democratic Party is full of young women. The party has also decided to form a committee for women's issues, which is working with the main party committee. I am co-chairing the committee."

Farida Naqash, one of the founder members of the *Tagammu'* party, commented on the party's vision on women's participation:

"We are the only party in Egypt which has an agglomeration of women. Within the party, there is a percentage for women in the general conference, the progressive women's union, in addition to allowing all the women that are members in political parties to run for elections for all positions. There are ten female members of the central committee that come from the general conference, in addition to electing new female members of this committee. Also, the progressive women's union is a semi-independent organization that has its own leadership. Its leader is a member of the higher party council. The women's union leadership is playing an important role in the political office of the party. We used the quota system since the establishment of the party, though the number of women in the party is still low."

The *Tagammu'* party has submitted a draft law stating the necessity of women's representation in nomination, with a minimum percentage of 30 percent (Islam Times). However, as Naqash also reported, even though the number of women in the party has increased after the revolution, it still remains lower than expected. Dalia Ziada, part of the women's committee of the *Adl* Party, which has seen a huge participation of middle-class women and housewives says:

"Most of the members of the party participated in the revolution, and they now recognize the important role

of women. Many housewives are in the party, and the
majority is practicing politics for the first time."
This can be exemplified indeed by Dina Wahba, a young activist
who entered politics for the first time after the revolution:

"I am a woman coordinator and I work in the women's commit-
tee of the Social Democratic Party. The committee includes pioneers
of the feminist movement both from the old and the new gener-
ations. However, when we try to push for an agenda, we find that the
party tries to direct us toward other issues that need to be handled."

Thus, political parties are unlikely to put women at the top of
their lists and back women's campaigns. At most, they only put
women on a separate committee, segregating them from other
committees and the mainstream work of the party. Also, two
women parties have been recently formed, although they have
not formally been registered yet. "The New Woman" party,
launched by the writer Reem Abu Eid, aims to combat discrimination against women during the current transition. The party
welcomes any woman or man of any ideology. The party aims
to review laws that have harmed women issued under the former regime, to protect women from any form of violence, and
to support rural women and marginalized groups, promoting
education and the eradication of illiteracy. However, the party,
according to its statement, wants to take a distance from other
feminist groups, which, according to the founder, did not benefit women at all. In addition, a new party called "Egyptian
Women" has been established, which aims at achieving social
justice for women. The party's main goals revolve around four
axes: political, developmental, social, and cultural. The party
aims to establish sustainable development projects in various
fields such as health, education, and agriculture. Although the
party has been announced in September and is still under formation, it has been welcomed by many prominent Egyptian
women.

Despite a lack of definite numbers and specific roles for women
in the current set of political parties after the revolution, it has
been estimated that there was a general increase in the number

of politically active women. However, not all women that are currently politically active have a feminist vision, as Khafagy explains:

"There are some divisions. Many young women who are politically active did not talk to us (the women's committee), saying that there are no particular issues concerning women. But I think that there are specific issues that need to be addressed separately. There are a few girls from the thawra *who are still not convinced about our requests, as they think that a discourse without women's issues is more politically attractive. But when you discuss it with them, they don't have logic for refusing that."*

For the first time in Egyptian history, one woman, Bothaina Kamel, an anchorwoman, is running for the presidency out of around eleven candidates.[35] Kamel does not consider herself a feminist but a woman from the *shaab*, "people," and thanks to her popularity, she is developing her candidacy and program:

"There has to be a practical example for women, especially because women have participated before, during, and after the revolution, whether in Tahrir Square, planning for the events, confronting bullets, and taking care of the injured people. By putting myself forward, I am making Egypt a real democratic country. When I first said that I was nominating myself, many were surprised and shocked by such a decision, but now they have begun to see me as a courageous candidate, as they know that I was among the protesters from the beginning."

When I asked her about her agenda, she replied:

"It doesn't matter to Egyptians whether someone is a woman or a man; what's important is whether it's someone who can understand and deliver. First of all, I didn't nominate myself just for Egyptian women, but for all the Arab Republic of Egypt, women and men. But considering myself a member of a neglected sector of the society, my concern would be intensified more for all the other neglected sectors and weak people: the Christians, the old age people, the women, the handicapped, the Nubians, and the Bedouins. I com-

pletely believe that working on elevating the position of women in Egypt will have its own impact on the whole society. That's why I chose the expression, 'My agenda is Egypt,' because I want people to understand that my main concern will be for Egypt. That's why I don't like to meet in fancy places, or hotels, but I prefer meeting Egyptians in their homes, factories, and in the slums." [36]

Even though Bothaina Kamel might undoubtedly be a charismatic leader, still, the majority of Egyptians are not prepared to accept a woman for this position. As Doaa Abdelaal from Iknowpolitics, explains:

"Kamel has potential as a candidate despite lacking a strong legacy among Egyptians. The presence of a female candidate is significant at this crucial junction in post-revolutionary Egypt."[37]

But as M.S., an assistant to the Mufti Ali Gomaa, explained, having women in positions of leadership does not go against the precepts of the *Shari'a,* and religion cannot be used by people as a pretext to explicate the political exclusion of women. Thus, the general denial of having a woman run for president could not be vindicated using Islam as justification, but it can be explained by looking at the social conservatism and overspread prejudice toward women.

"Women can work in almost all positions except for the Welayah Ammah (Khalifa of all Muslims). Women cannot take over the ruling of all Muslims, but they can take positions like the presidency, ministers, or managing an institution. The Khalifa is on behalf of the prophet, and he is responsible for the whole Islamic country. The president is a different shape of ruling and can be represented by a woman." [38]

The same opinion is shared by Khaled Hamza, leader of the Muslim Brotherhood and editor of its official website, who believe in the freedom for women to nominate themselves in the elections. However, he says, the Muslim Brotherhood will not vote for a woman running for president of the country.

But despite their active role in street demonstrations and the slight increment of women in political parties, at a governmental level, women have obviously been confined to the sidelines.

A declining tendency toward women's representation in the political transition especially interested the newly appointed ministers. The new government of Essam Sharaf appointed only one woman to his cabinet of twenty-six ministers, nominating Fayza Abu El Naga as minister of international cooperation.[39] For women activists, another disappointment has been the failure to select women as leaders of the governorates. The delusion came after the prime minister's announcement that there would be no appointment of female governors (ECWR 2011). In addition, it is still unclear how many seats will be designated for women in the new Parliament, which consists of the People's Assembly (the lower house) and the *Shura* Council (the Upper House). Article 38 of the Constitutional Declaration states that the law that "regulates the right of candidacy to the People's Assembly and *Shura* Council in accordance with the electoral system and may include a minimum participation of women in both chambers." However, no specific number is reported (Equality Now 2011). Recently, the government has agreed on two draft laws regarding the People's Assembly and *Shura* Council and elections. The amendments include granting a seat for women in the first half of the political parties' lists, which would put women's representation at 20 percent at least [40] (ECWR 2011). However, it seems that the political parties still refuse to place women on their election lists and to allocate specific seats to women. The new electoral law is very difficult to understand and does not clarify the position of women in the list. The law also canceled the women's quota system; the quota for workers and farmers is instead maintained (Sharp 8, 2011). Although the quota system did increase women's representation in the Parliament, this also ensured further power and more seats to the National Democratic Party, boosting the general opposition to the introduction of this law. Women's groups and activists members of NGOs are currently divided about its removal. For some, despite the fact that the law increased the number of NDP members in Parliament, this does not reduce the importance of the law as a success for women's rights and it should be maintained in the current period. While these quotas were criticized for being yet another vehicle for ensuring power to the ruling NDP to dominate parliament rather than advancing women's rights, a reformed quota system would have been a positive step in Egypt's political development. In our recent discussion, Khafagy highlighted the importance of maintaining a quota system, though she favors a proportional list system in which each party would field a minimum number of female candidates as part of its electoral slate. She says:

"There are different kinds of quotas. We want to have women in the proportional list. But people still link the quota to the past regime, when they increased the number of women to actually support the number of NDP members."

Also for Dalia Ziada and Dina Wahba, it is important to maintain the system at this stage, since society still sees women as politically inexpert. As Ziada explains:

"The quota gives women the chance to prove themselves in these positions. Women will never succeed in politics waiting for people to vote for them."

However, for many other experts in the field, the maintenance of a quota for women in Parliament will not be necessary in a new democratic Egypt. The judge Tahani El Gebali released a statement in which she stated that:

"The mature political situation experienced by the Egyptian people now requires them to abandon the concept of quota and leave the seats in parliament to the choice of the voters. A quota cannot be accepted after the success of the revolution and the emergence of popular awareness and full recognition of women's role in the revolution. And our aspiration of achieving true democracy and justice requires us to reconsider the quota system. History has shown us how the rights of workers and peasants have been lost in the presence of a quota for workers and peasants in the People's Assembly and Shura Council" (Abdel Hamid Hafez 2011).

Furthermore, a former symbol of the regime and one of the first entities to receive harsh criticism after the revolution was the National Council for Women (NCW), for which a future structure remains unclear. Created by presidential decree in 2000, the NCW acted as the official entity for the advancement of women's rights in the country, and it was presided over by Mrs. Suzanne Mubarak. The government of Sharaf has been considering which shape the women's mechanism should adopt. The transitional government considered the idea of establishing a women's commission to operate under the prime minister's office or the creation of a Ministry for Women's Affairs (Rashuan 2011). However, it seems that the prime minister took back his decision to name the national women's mechanism as a commission in response to the demands of female activists who opposed the formation of a commission and rather called for a strong national women's machinery and the establishment of a Ministry for Women's Affairs. The cabinet has been also considering the establishment of a separate body for women and children's matters, having a legal entity upon which a resolution shall be made by the Supreme Council of the Armed Forces. As Khafagy explains:

"There are no serious steps toward its restructure, there is no transparency, they refused a minister for women, and they want to have a commission. But they did not say what they mean for commission, who the coordinators are. Until now there was no transparency about this issue."

The NCW recently became a victim of negative propaganda asking for its dissolution. Some movements are asking for the abolishment or modification of some laws concerning family matters that can be ascribed among the successes achieved by the NCW and the National Council for Childhood and Motherhood (NCCM). Therefore, there might be a major setback in bringing forward women's agenda if any of those calls succeed in framing the laws that protect women rights as merely laws initiated by the old regime, and challenging their legitimacy.

3.5 Back to an old Egypt: the case of March 8

Because of this initial exclusion of women from the table of the political discussion, the Nawal El Saadawi group, several NGOs, and newly formed coalitions called for a *"Millioneya* March" on March 8 to remind Egypt of women's role in the revolution, to protest against the choice of the Constitutional Committee to leave out women from the discussion of the constitutional reforms, and to protest against the new article stating that the president should be male and not married to a foreign woman. The initiative was totally independent and no political parties were involved in it. The main idea of the event, as Ms. Nehad Abol Komsan explained, was that of:

"Celebrating all martyrs, men and women, and to remind society of the role women played during the revolution."[41]

In addition, women activists also wanted to demonstrate against the disappointing decision of excluding women from all decision-making processes, as well as ask for equal legislation and for the criminalization of violence against women. The last and most controversial demand was mainly about women's right to run for president. As a consequence of these demands and the perceived notion by males of the "hijacking" and dividing of the political reforms being demanded, female protestors

were met with chants of "Not now," "No to women, yes to FGM," and *"Al shaab yoreed esqat al madam"* ("the people demand the removal of the lady/woman"), as well as violent actions (Naib 2011). Most of them said that where a man did not succeed, a woman won't either. Besides, some men were frustrated at the idea of having a march only for women, arguing there should be unity and not divisions after the revolution. Others, after having seen several foreign women attend the march, accused women of having a Western agenda, representing the interests of the former first lady, and working for foreign organizations. Following the events, even some of the participants and organizers recognized some of the errors of the demonstration. Even though they all agree on the necessity of having the event, some also had critical opinions about its organization. Azza Kamel, founder of the Women's Research Centre, said:

"I see that it was important for women to protest and that's why I participated. However, there was bad management. I don't judge the idea itself. Sincerely, when I read the slogan asking for women's candidacy in the presidential elections, I considered it an exaggerating, provocative claim in such a time. However, after all, everyone is free to express what he/she wants."[42]

As for the identity of those involved in the clashes, opinions diverge. According to Hennawy, those in Tahrir were clearly from the Salafist group; for Bothaina Kamel instead:

"These were not the same men that made the revolution with us, but they have been paid to create chaos and instability."

Even though there were several other demonstrations in downtown Cairo that day, as Sholkamy pointed out: "No other demonstrators were heckled, told that their demands are unjustified, unnecessary, a threat to the gains of the revolution, out of time, out of place, and/or the product of a 'foreign agenda'! No other demonstrators were told to 'go back home and to the kitchen'! No others were heckled for how they looked and what they were wearing" (Sholkamy 2011). What happened also raised the question of the extent to which the Egyptian population is ready to accept women in leadership positions and how it views women groups in the country.

Even for Khaled Hamza:

"This aggression, as well as any other cases of harassment in the streets, is not related to religion. This aggression was made by people who have been overpowered for too long and are now trying to repress the weakest sectors of the society".

Fatema Khafagy and Doaa Abdelaal, also try to regard what happened positively. For Khafagy:

"It was a good thing, in the end, as I understood that we need to be more organized and stand together. We need to talk to other people and try to convince them. But we cannot deal with the ultra-conservatism. They came to scare us."

And also for Abdelaal:

"I was harassed but I was happy, because this was the first time to have people with banners, calling for their rights."

However, many have argued that the inspirational images of gender solidarity in Tahrir Square in the early days of Egypt's revolution soon gave way to a wide-ranging patriarchal mentality and the conservative beliefs of Egyptian society. This is also because another case of violence was reported only one day later. On March 9, the Egyptian military rounded up scores of female protesters, subjecting many of them to virginity tests and threatening them with prostitution charges. Women also claimed to have been beaten and given electric shocks. An Egyptian general who confirmed the case said that the tests were conducted so that the women would not be able to assert that they had been sexually abused by the military. "We didn't want them to say we had sexually assaulted or raped them, so we wanted to prove that they weren't virgins in the first place," the general said. "None of them were [virgins]." He added, "The girls who were detained were not like your daughter or mine... These were girls who had camped out in tents with male protesters in Tahrir Square, and we found ... Molotov cocktails and [drugs]" (Rice 2011). The abuse of the women caused anger, and activists and youth groups held a demonstration to press military leadership to investigate soldiers. However, as Dalia Ziada explains:

"We should differentiate between the SCAF and the army. The SCAF is the leading power now, and they have to rule with a different mentality because they are ruling civilians. I respect them; I know they have good intentions, and I know they want to support women. However, they have failed to prove that they are pro-women's rights. They are dealing only with men, and all the people they are addressing in any decision-making process are men. We can understand that because before they did not have any access to common citizens, and because they are a masculine authority."

A similar idea is shared by the journalist Myriam Zaki, who says that

"The army is a conservative institution and is gender-blind. The

army has its own psychology and, for the first time in many years, the army is dealing with civilians. The virginity tests were a good test for the army, in order to test the ground, to see the reaction of NGOs and the international community. And this is healthy."[43]

Perhaps partially due to the accusations directed at it, the SCAF released a decree on March 31 that amended seven articles in the penal code and enforced severe punishment for sexual harassment. Following the revision, Article 267 now states that those found guilty of raping women will face a life sentence or the death penalty. An additional clause in Article 268 stipulates that whoever commits an assault or threat or is involved in any way in such acts of aggression faces a minimum prison sentence of seven years. In addition, Article 269 stipulates that public verbal abuse is punishable with a three-month prison sentence along with a fine of 300 Egyptian pounds (Abdoun 2011).

3.6 Claiming their space: the revival of gender-based coalitions and groups

Immediately after the revolution, women activists created strong coalitions and new groups in order to defend women's rights and propose their ideas for equal participation in the political process to the representatives of the state. As Margot Badran argues, Egyptian women are now engaging in the same multi-level activism of Sha'rawi's Feminist Union, fighting for their rights while working simultaneously within the framework of post-revolution movements (Badran 2011). On February 22, a few days after the end of the revolution, more than one hundred NGOs involved in women and development, legal studies, and human rights announced the establishment of "The Egyptian Coalition for Civic Education and Participation of Women," led by the ECWR. The goal of the coalition is to spread awareness of democratization in Egypt, underlining the importance of women's role in achieving social and political change. The coalition, thanks to the geographical diversity of its members, aims to spread the principles of education, civic culture, and women's rights all over the country in light of the upcoming elections (Nabil 2011). So far, "The Egyptian Coalition for Civic Education and Participation of Women" has been active in hosting workshops and debates about the political participation of women in the transitional period, also preparing petitions for the SCAF and organizing demonstrations. A second important group of NGOs clustered around the "Nazra" Association for Feminist Studies and the Alliance of Arab Women (AAW). This independent group includes eleven[44] already-established women's NGOs that are currently focusing on women's rights in the Constitution during the transitional period. This group has especially demonstrated a definite refusal of the illegitimate role of the NCW and its representation of Egyptian women, calling for its dissolution in a public statement. As Khafagy puts it:

"Before the revolution, we used to work individually, but now we think that numbers are power. The military and the prime minister are now afraid of numbers."

She also explains that not all women in this group are working on the same issues. Some are working in the field of electoral law, while other members have a much more feminist approach. If these two coalitions mainly include gender experts in the field of women's rights, a more variegated and people-based group seems to be the "Coalition of the Revolutionary Women." This coalition includes single individuals or experts from civil society organizations who think that the revolution brought a backlash to women's rights in the country, in terms of political participation and representation. Its main approach is that of organizing seminars, workshops and conferences to debate the current situation for women in post-revolutionary Egypt.

But despite strong activism on the ground in recent demonstrations, as Dina Abou El Soud, leader and activist of the coalition, explains, being neither a political party nor an NGO, it lacks funds to operate concretely and has so far remained at the level of an advocacy organization. [45] She discloses that the relationship between groups and/or women NGOs is defined more by competition than cooperation. Groups are left to fight and compete among themselves for funds and protect their interests, rather than to work together toward a common goal. Unfortunately, this harms the civil society system as a whole, despite it being composed of excellent NGOs.

Many other groups working for the cause of women also started to proliferate on the Internet.[46] On Facebook, several new groups have appeared, like SAWA (previously called Egyptian Women for Change), which has 532 members. SAWA considers itself an independent, non-affiliated, Egyptian women's rights group of advocates. The mission is advocacy for the inclusion and engagement of women in rebuilding the nation. The activities of the group include media monitoring, encouraging more gender-sensitive media, raising awareness of women's issues with fledgling political parties, and encouraging parties to put women on their agendas from the outset. But SAWA also wants to take a new, social-based approach. As Hennawi, one of its members and leaders says:

"We need to change the direction of the women's movement. Now when women talk, they should not speak only about their problems, but about society as a whole, and adopt the problems of society. She should not go out only to defend herself, but to defend society, and only in this case will they admit her requests. In order for women to achieve an equal status, when they are asking about their rights, this should sound like an achievement for the whole society."

And for Dalia Ziada:

"Women's organizations have always tried to give a feminine impression. The big mistake of these groups is in the fact that they have never dealt with women's issues as a social problem, but they always stressed on women-only problems, like alimony, dowry, and

divorce. These things are only partial and not major social problems."
However, so far, the group has mainly engaged in organizing
gender trainings and round-table discussions, and its membership remains limited to gender activists and feminists.

A significant achievement was realized on June 4, when the
Arab Alliance for Women (AAW) organized a convention during which a "Women's Charter" document was created.[47] The
conference gathered thousands of women and men in order to
discuss the points of the charter and priorities in the Constitution. The charter was finalized and ratified by 500 NGOs,
3,200 women and men from all twenty-seven governorates,
and 500,000 signatures from the local level to the governorate
level. The charter includes seven kinds of demands and issues
related to the political representation of women, social and
economic rights, the future of the National Women's Machinery, women's appointment to judiciary posts, and the role of
media. The charter has been presented to the government, but
any kind of feedback was provided by the decision makers, and
it rests to be seen which practical and concrete consequences it
will have for the lives of Egyptian women.[48]

Indeed, despite the fact that women's membership in different
coalitions and women groups has absolutely increased after the
revolution, in several cases activities mainly remain anchored
to debates, recommendations, preparatory meetings, and online social networking activities. The type of women's organizations that emerged after the revolution continued to be
avowedly feminist or semi-feminist in orientation and made up
largely of women of the *petite bourgeoisie* and upper-class. Even
though women activists and NGOs are strongly lobbying for
the woman's cause, so far, however, they have not succeeded
in influencing the procedures of the new government, either in
terms of numerical representation or policies. Various reasons
remain for the lack of resonance that these groups have with
society. This can be explained by the lack of constituency for
these groups at the level of the masses, and for their scarce
engagement with youth and non-secular women. Furthermore,

there is still not something like a single and homogenous move-ment. There are many active women's groups and/or NGOs who at some point work together. As some secular women activ-ists have argued, a unified movement that would bring together secular and Islamist women is absolutely not on the agenda. Hence, as Dr. Tadros upholds:

"The movement of women does not have alliances and does not have a constituency. By alliances, I mean that you are able to find people in the society who are sympathetic with your cause or can support you, like the students in Cairo University, with which the women movement did not engage. I think you need to have a united women movement that also focuses on "social justice issues." [49]

And M. S., assistant of Mufti Ali Gomaa:

"The success of these groups is very limited. The Egyptian so-ciety is religious by nature, and when they try to send a message, it needs to be sent through religion."

Alia Dawood also underlines their scarce sense of unity. Accord-ing to Dawood, during reign of the past regime, women leaders of different groups, coalitions and/or NGOs were competing for funds and media attention. She believes that this trend has not yet ended. Additionally, the stigma of having somehow been as-sociated with Suzanne Mubarak's policies still remains a reason for the general social rejection of these groups.

"We don't have the kind of movement made by groups that try to achieve something together and have the same goals. There are sev-eral women who are presidents and chairs of these NGOs, and they find it unacceptable that only one of them should be the leader of the movement; there is a lot of competition. They compete for fund-ing, for media attention, even in their relationship with the former regime. They also have contacts at the grassroots level, but it is more of a top-down approach. I think that the feminists that are around right now are not the ones that are going to change anything. We need another generation of young girls to come in." [50]

The same concept is reiterated by Doaa Abdelaal, who refers to the "NGO-ization" of the women's movement. [51] She thinks that:

"Because of the wrong approach that women's organizations had before the revolution, women have not been recognized as powerful agents of change, because for so many years they reduced their focus to talking about issues like family laws. Egypt doesn't have a movement, it has NGOs, and we have an NGO-ization of the women movement. They didn't have a legacy among the people. If you see someone like Gamila Ismail, who has been active in the streets for many years, you will find that she has a strong legacy in the streets because she has been an activist; now people listen to her. Many other women were sitting beside the first lady too. So now we have this threat that whatever has been achieved is corrupted and affiliated with the old regime. After the revolution, and looking at the different coalitions, I think that they are still going on the some hoops that they have been going on for years. What we need to see are NGOs that reflect the needs of the people. However, so far, they continue to focus their efforts in sending petitions without understanding that this is a military and conservative system."

Also, Dalia Ziada seconds Abdelaal by saying:

"We need to support the grassroots, helping them to understand their rights. The first thing is making coalitions among women's groups and non-women's groups and joining forces. It is important to have coalitions, but we need to have clear vision on what we want to achieve for women in at least five years time. Many groups of women lack this vision."

And the same for the journalist Myriam Zaki:

"Women need to push for a social justice agenda and not only for an exclusive agenda. They need to push for inclusiveness."

Of a different opinion seems to be Imen Bibars, who does not believe in the necessity of having a unified movement, and indeed she argues:

"Several organizations work in different areas and have different ideologies. We need to come together for the most important things. People are all coming now and asking, 'Why don't you work together?' Why should I work in sixteen areas? We work in different areas and we have different goals. When we need to do something to-

gether, we are together. The real problem is with the donors. People are changing because of the money."

Azza Kamel also specifies:

"There is not a feminist movement. There are two kinds of organizations that we can define feminist. The first one is the 'new women's foundation.' The rest are organizations working in women's issues but without a clear feminist vision."

As a result, in order for the women's movement to survive and be socially accepted, it will be fundamental to equate women's requests to the broader cause of social justice and democratization to avoid labeling their demands as gender-driven. In the coming period, women groups will need to stop to address women's issues as a "special case". Furthermore, women's coalitions will need to expand their constituencies targeting women from the lower classes, supporting their real needs of employment, education and dignity. Finally, any future women activism should be based on the same cultural beliefs of the masses, and locally grounded with a vision through which social relations are organized.

3.7 An emerging force: women of the Muslim Brotherhood

On July 1, for the first time in sixty years, the Muslim Sisterhood held an enormous conference. The meeting was attended by hundreds of female members of the Muslim Brotherhood and saw the participation of the granddaughters of Hassan Al-Banna, the founder of the group, and the wives of the group's leaders. The conference, titled "Women from Revolution to Renaissance," discussed the important role of women during the uprisings and in the reconstruction of the new Egypt. Muslim Brotherhood leaders such as Mahmoud Ezzat, the deputy leader, and Mahmoud Hussein, the secretary general, emphasized the significant role that women have inside the movement, which seems to have the largest representation of women of all the political groups. However, so far, the group has not made a final decision as to what role will be assigned to women inside the party during the transition. Still, the Muslim Brotherhood's newly formed Freedom and Justice Party is conducting a survey to decide whether to integrate women in leadership positions inside the group or not (Elyan 2011).

The Muslim Brotherhood was founded in 1928 by the teacher Hassan Al-Banna, who originally initiated the movement under the framework of a charity organization. The Brotherhood continued to focus on outreach and missionary activities (*dawa*) even after the murder of its leader in 1949, continuing to attract millions of adepts. As Khaled Hamza says:

"The strength of this movement was coming from its understanding of Egyptian society. The Muslim Brotherhood combined the needs of Egyptian society, Sufi roots, and moderate Egyptian Islam."

Hassan Al-Banna supported the formation of a Muslim Sisters group, which began its activities in 1932 and was initially led by Labiba Ahmed. The "Society of Muslim Women," led by Zeinab al-Ghazali, a prominent Islamic leader, instead remained independent from the Sisterhood. Al-Ghazali only became politically involved in the movement, assisting the families of those jailed, after Nasser began to repress the Muslim Brotherhood. Despite being partially tolerated under Sadat as a counter force against socialists, under Mubarak, on the contrary, the movement was forcefully banned. The government continued to impede free access to political activity for the movement, using the Emergency Law to crack down on terrorist activities of fundamentalist Islamist groups. However, although officially outlawed, the movement continued to exist as the strongest political alternative to the National Democratic Party (Tadros 2011, 89). Although it continued to be mainly committed to providing social assistance, the movement achieved a major political success in 2005 when independents won eighty-eight seats in the new Parliament.

The Muslim Brotherhood itself, as well as the Sisterhood, has always proposed an antagonistic vision of women's roles in society in comparison to the views expressed by secular women groups. The female members of the Brotherhood, taking from Hassan Al-Banna's "Letter of the Muslim Woman" (*resalet al mar'a al muslima'*), emphasize the role of caretaker (mother and wife) given to women to proceed on the right path in Islamic society. However, recently, Islamic feminism has been silently reinventing itself. Some female Islamists have started a gender-friendly re-interpretation of Islamic sources, searching in the *Qura'n* and *Sunna* for the source for women's emancipation (Wild 2011).

The movement of the Muslim Brotherhood has often taken contentious perspectives over the political and social roles of women in society, clashing with the government, which the Brotherhood accuses of hampering Egyptian traditions through foreign impositions of Western ideas.[52] In 2007, the Brotherhood released a crucial draft party platform, which soon raised public concerns and criticism. For liberal and secular women, the Brotherhood did not value women's role and capabilities of, keeping them in a subordinate position. The contested statement says: "Duties and responsibilities assumed by the head of state, such as army commanding, are in contradiction with the socially acceptable roles for women" (Eft 45-46, 2011). The draft also stated that senior leadership roles in the government should only be for Muslims, excluding the possibility of having a Christian Copt for president.[53] The clause cast the organization in the middle of internal debates between the moderate wing, mainly composed by younger members, and the most conservative one. Since then, the young members of the Brotherhood, both women and men, started to use social networks to make their opinions heard by the old leadership (Abdel-Latif 20, 2008). As Abdel Rahman Ayyash explains:

"Women inside the MB are divided into two groups: one is asking for more rights while the other uses a sexist interpretation, arguing that women cannot be empowered to the level of men. But the first group is a minority, mostly formed by youth who are pushing for women's participation."

Politically, the Brotherhood has also occasionally supported the candidacies of women in local districts, such as Jihan al-Halafawi and Makarem al-Deeri (Eft 61, 2011). One of the pretexts that senior leaders of the Brotherhood often used to deny women's participation was related to the risk of being harassed or perhaps detained by police forces.

However, since the revolution, women became even more restless with their unequal status, seeking ways to affirm their demands for more representation inside the movement and to cover a formal consultative position. This renewal is proposed by the younger generations, daughters and sons of senior Brotherhood leaders [54] (Abdel Latif 1, 2011). Typical is the case of Ayyash Abdel Rahman, and Sarah Mohammed, a mass communication graduate student and daughter of prominent Brotherhood leaders who joined the group at age seventeen. About the Brotherhood, Ayyash says:

"The Brotherhood doesn't have the easiest attitude towards women. In the hierarchal system, there are several positions for men but just two for women.[55] Women cannot participate in any elections inside the Brotherhood. Only a few figures inside the Brotherhood are women, like Jihan al-Halafawy. They think that a woman cannot lead the country. However, they have recently changed their idea about having a woman for president, and recently they revised their statement. The Brotherhood understood that they need to put more women at the top level of the bureau. Security issues are over now, and they can't have any justification for that."

And he continues:

"They cannot be the leaders of the movement, and they are not free voters. I think that having women empowered within the Brotherhood is important and comes from the same ideas of Al-Banna."

Khaled Hamza has a different opinion, and he highlights the gendered renewal of the movement post-revolution:

"I think that in this period, after the removal of the Mubarak regime, there will be a massive change, and there will be more space for the sisters, like, for example, giving them the possibility of being elected in the Shura Council."

Sarah, on the contrary, stresses on the unchanged, contradictory attitude of the Brotherhood toward women's issues:

"If you talk with the leaders about the future of women in the movement, they give you good answers, telling you that women have the right to participate. You will also find a good program, but it won't be applied. It is just theoretical. The Brotherhood seems to have a problem with the women and youth component."

On recent occasions, the Muslim Brotherhood has been often politically associated with most conservative groups, like the Salafis, for sharing some restrictive views, especially concerning the Personal Status Laws. However, the Brotherhood prefers not to be confused with the other Islamist factions in order to keep unaltered its reputation of being a moderate movement. For Sarah:

"The Salafis are a real problem, saying that women should stay at home and go out only for emergency reasons. The Jamah Islameyya should be neglected. You need to preach the right Islam and the correct Islamic rules. Religion gives women all their rights and supports the participation of women." [56]

And Ayyash:

"I don't think that the Brotherhood will make positive gains from this coalition, as I think that the Salafis will corrupt some of their ideas."

The same feeling is shared by Khaled Hamza:

"The Brotherhood and the Salafis are very different in their

views on women. The Salafi movement has a limited view of women, due to the Wahabi interpretation, which is not in Egyptian nature. I see that pushing women behind their veils is equal to isolating them from society."

In a trial, to have a status of political acceptance, the Muslim Brotherhood assured that the recent amendments made to the Freedom and Justice Party platform focused on two key points, which are the possibility of nominating Copts or women to the presidency. The Freedom and Justice Party announced that it is not against women holding high-ranking positions, yet it does not think that women are suitable for the presidential office. These pro-women's representation names includes Ibrahim Al-Zaafarani, Abdel-Monem Abul-Futuh[57], and Essam al-Erayan, who have constantly pushed for women to be included in the Brotherhood's highest power structures and voiced criticism against the movement's veto on female presidential candidates (Abdel Latif 2, 2011). However, other leaders remain outspoken against many existing pro-women laws in Egypt. But for Khaled Hamza, the revolution changed the way the Brotherhood looks at women. The conference of the Sisters is a clear signal of a new genuine attitude of the Brotherhood. In this regard, he says:

"I think this conference was held to express how the Brother-hood thinks after the revolution. The Brotherhood is going to have a massive change in their policy toward male youth and sisters."

But the majority of secular activists remain skeptical about the Brotherhood's declarations. For both Azza Kamel and Dalia Ziada, the Brotherhood is playing a new power game, trying to appear as a renovated democratic force. Kamel says:

"They are smarter now because they are pushing women. They want power and they are opportunistic."

And for Ziada:

"Now they are planning according to the new rules of the game. They want to look more democratic."

However, for Dina Wahba, the Brotherhood is playing a safe card by supporting women's political participation:

"Women from the Brotherhood are empowered, and they are

the model that society wants. I just met a woman from the Brotherhood; she is seventeen, she speaks English, and we talked about gender issues. I am sure that ten years from now, the Brotherhood will look extremely different, especially in the participation of women. The new generations are different. If you have a girl of seventeen who is speaking on behalf of the Brotherhood, it means that they are investing in women more than any other political parties. It seems that finally, they are empowering their women."

As Wild also says, the revolution allowed space in a fertile time for a renovated form of Islamic feminism. A few months from now, there will be proof of what the Brotherhood is really pushing for. The kind of gender balance that the Brotherhood will introduce among its ranks will be a sign of the real direction that the movement is taking. Playing the gender card might be perhaps the smarter move the movement could make in order to renovate its image, avoid tiring the group, and look democratic in the international arena.

3.8 Suzanne Mubarak like Jihan Sadat: clashes over the Personal Status Laws

The events of March 8 have perhaps represented the start of another significant controversy between women's groups and conservative Islam. Because Egyptian history seems to repeat itself, clashes over the Personal Status Laws immediately emerged after the revolution, restarting an ancient fight between Islamists and women's groups. In the current transition, women not only have been put on the sidelines of the political decision-making process, but some of their personal and family rights have also been seriously jeopardized.

Since the time of Hoda Sha'rawi and even before, feminists, women's groups, and activists have called for a more gender-equal re-interpretation of the *Shari'a* law, which has been unalterably the source of family laws during the last century. Over the years, some improvements in the laws have been attained, which, however, have not disturbed the patriarchal family model (Badran 2011). The reformed laws introduced under Mubarak were the *khul'* law (the unilateral divorce of women upon renouncing to their right of alimony and the dowry), amendments to the custody law and nationality law, raising the legal age of marriage from sixteen to eighteen for both boys and girls, as well as the introduction in 2004 of specialized courts for family problems. Although these laws have been directly associated with the first lady, they have been primarily the product of years of efforts by women's NGOs for which Mrs. Mubarak provided the final seal. With the end of the Mubarak era, these laws started to carry the stigma of the old regime, personifying Suzanne Mubarak and the entourage of the NCW. However, as Khafagy explains, these laws have been the fruits of lobbying of women's NGOs, and should not carry either the name or discredit of the first lady:

"These are not laws of Suzanne Mubarak. These are the laws that many women's groups and several NGOs pushed for introduction, and this is documented historically. Suzanne Mubarak has been the port parole, *as she was the first lady. Changes have been made accurately by NGOs. We have been lobbying, proposed studies, and convinced people for the last ten years. It was really the work of women activists and not of Suzanne Mubarak. She only had the authority to speak to the Parliament and had the power to pass these laws, and this is something that I keep explaining."*

For Dawood, what is happening to Suzanne Mubarak is an exact reappearance of what already occurred during Jihan Sadat. For Dawood, the egotism and the misuse of the Personal Status Laws have been seen by many as symbols of the omnipresence of the first lady and the desire of the regime to appease the West and its democratic standards. In this regard, she upholds that:

"If you see the way these laws were presented in the media, it looked like Suzanne Mubarak equaled women's rights. And the introduction of these laws was very similar to the introduction of many other laws, and there was this association between a deeply heated regime and women's rights. They looked like they were imposed on

people by the first lady, and this turned people against women's rights. Now that she is gone, they want to go back and remove every-thing she has done because she abused her power and because they feel that she has been trying to please the West."

Indeed, between April and May, several protests have been staged by Islamic movements such as the Salafis and newly formed groups like "Saving the Family" and "Egypt's Men Revolution" [58] (Awadalla). Demonstrators, mainly fathers dragged by Islamists into the protests, have gathered on several occasions during the last few months in front of the Ministry of Justice, Al-Azhar, and the Journalist Syndicate in order to protest against those that have been nicknamed the "Suzanne Mubarak Laws." The initial protests have been addressing especially Law No.4 of 2005, according to which the period of child custody for both boys and girls with the mother is set until the age of fifteen. A divorced woman has the right to live in the marital home with the children until the time of *hadāna* (custody) ends or the husband should provide to her another place to stay with her children. However, if she remarries, she loses their custody (Bernard-Maugiron 2010, 22). According to the protesters, divorced fathers can only see their children for three hours per week in a public place. Hence, the protests called for changing the visiting time from three hours to at least forty-eight hours a week and changing the age of mother's custody to nine years for girls and seven years for boys (Awadalla). Ali Gomaa, the grand *mufti* of Al-Azhar, promised to call for the amendment of the Personal Status Laws in regard to the custody of children according to religious jurisprudence by saying that he will announce a new *fatwa* that is fair to fathers (Fahmy b). Also, the justice minister's deputy has also announced that the custody law will be amended by also banning the travel of children from divorced parents unless both parents consent. Both Nehad Abol Komsan, chair of ECWR, and Mohasen Saber, director of "Radio Motallaqat," go beyond any religious justification raised by these groups, arguing instead how practical and economic reasons are the real issues pertaining to the question. For Abol Komsan:

"These fathers cannot convince me that they like to wake up at 6 a.m., feed and wash the baby, and bring him to school and wait until he finishes school. They will have to leave their work and go to take the baby after school. This is nothing more than an economic issue. These fathers want back their flat in order to start another life with another woman. They simply want to throw their kids to other women. They will leave the kids with their mothers or with a new wife. For some women it can be an economic issue as well, as she needs alimony and the flat. But for many other women, kids represent a project of life. The union that exists between mother and kids does not exist with the fathers."

And Mohasen Saber:

"I agree with them on demanding an extension of the visiting hours, but I disagree on changing the age of custody. This is only because the alimony to the ex-wife and child cuts half of their salaries."[59]

Interesting to note has also been the massive participation of Salafi women, who have marched and demonstrated against family laws beside men. As in 1985, the fact that the attack to these laws also comes from many Muslim women who stand to benefit from it remains highly significant. This underlines, once again, the inner divisions that remain between secular and the most conservative Islamist women, and the constant tensions that remain among these groups. Islamist women have especially been attacking the *khul'* law, which they say has corrupted family relations and increased divorce rates. Chancellor Mohammed Bakr also announced the intention of the "Save the Egyptian Family" association to file a lawsuit to abolish the National Council for Women and the National Council for Motherhood and Childhood and to return to the original application of the Islamic *Shari'a* (Ali 2011).

But for Khafagy, this discourse does not make any sense, as these laws already derive from the *Shari'a* law:

"The family law is the only law based on Shari'a. So every time that we want to amend the family laws, it seems that we want to change the Shari'a law. In other countries, there are different and perhaps more flexible interpretations. Here they are insisting on the very conservative interpretations of the Shari'a. The inferior role of women became social belief of the people; it became part of the culture."

M.S. tries to interpret the events in this way:

"Personal Status Laws are those laws that control the relationships between people. Religion is integrating or interfering in these relationships, as religion is the one that tells what is forbidden, allowed, and acceptable. The Islamic Shari'a organizes the relationships between people. The women's rights groups want to raise their demands to a higher level, and that's why they come into a clash with the Islamic scholars, because for some scholars, according to their interpretation, some of these demands do not bring more rights to women."

The attempts to cancel and/or amend these laws worried women activists, who immediately sought to counter these efforts through debates and petitions. While many are trying to repeal these laws, other advocates gathered in front of the Al-Azhar Islamic Research Centre (IRC) to protest against any amendments. Fawzia Abdel-Sattar, a law professor at Cairo University and a former member of the People's Assembly, explains that the Personal Status Laws introduced under the Mubarak regime all derive from *Shari'a* law, and that it is unnecessary to blame the former first lady for their introduction (Leila 2011). Activists recognized the mistake of the old regime of having introduced these laws without an accurate legislative process and having imposed these laws on society as a whole. However, they also recognize the laws' importance for the promotion of women's rights and status in society. Some activists and experts have also advanced a political explanation to clarify the apparently scarce consideration that the government has toward women's groups' requests for not amending the current Personal Status Laws. For the activist Dina Abou El Soud, for example:

"The Brotherhood and the Salafis want to get rid of women because it is easier to attack women instead of fighting the liberals and the communists."

Khafagy's view is much more oriented toward political planning and she says:

"Women's rights have become nothing more than a card played by both the military council and the Islamists. The ruling military council is collaborating with the Muslim Brotherhood, using women's issues as a way of appeasing and extracting assurances from the latter."

Also, Professor Tadros has a political and power-based explanation for this. Referring to Foucault's analysis, there exist certain power relations between feminists, Islamists, and the state in Egypt. Power oscillates from one to the other in a series of reactions and counter-reactions and resistance to each other (Karam 1998, 4). Resistance to secularism and to women's organizations became equated with the preservation of existing gender relations, which means the perpetuation of patriarchal control and the maintenance of a certain social status quo. [60] This is indeed underlined by Tadros when she says:

"By liberating women, Islamists feel a threat to the status quo. In order to maintain social stability, they should maintain gender hierarchy."

Now, as in the past, the issue of the family laws constitutes a sort of collective awakening for women's groups and organizations in Egypt. The debates highlight certain realities within Egyptian society and politics that had been evolving gradually over many years. The most dominant and significant of these is the extent to which Islam has become the central feature of almost any discourse involving political, social, cultural, and economic change. In a country where a large majority of the population (85 percent) believes that Islam has a positive influence on Egyptian politics and 95 percent say it's good that Islam plays a large role in politics, clearly, women's rights should be once more compromised (Reuters 2011). According to the political path that the new government will take, women's organizations will understand whether or not they can count on the secular authoritarianism of the state to back them. However, for now, secular laws are no longer socially or legally accepted, as women's issues are greatly connected to the culture, especially in the Middle East. Therefore, Islamic law reform in regard to matters of personal status is the only socially accepted means to achieving goals that are relatively close to feminist demands in Egypt.

3.9 Sub-conclusion

This chapter, after having proposed a background analysis of the causes that led to the revolution of January 25, has focused its attention on the gendered aspects of the transition to democracy in Egypt by looking at the interaction between women's groups and politics in terms of relations with the state and political parties. After their strong involvement in street demonstrations during the eighteen days of the revolution, women have recognized the need to ensure that gender issues are placed on the agenda of the transition. However, the transition to a real democracy seems uncertain as women have begun to be excluded from the highest levels of decision making for the reform processes currently underway. Women were celebrated for their role in the revolution but they were immediately sidelined by all political forces in post-revolution political scene. As the comparative analysis proposed in the second chapter suggests, this seems to be a typical trend for post-revolutionary and transitional countries.

Hence, women's groups (feminist or pseudo-feminist) in Egypt have been left with the choice that has been summed up as the dilemma of "autonomy" versus "integration" (Waylen 1994, 339). However, following a century-long process, women's groups and activists from NGOs are failing to engage politically and to unify themselves around nationwide priorities and a common discourse. Besides, as some experts interviewed for this work have reported, the relationship between women's groups is still defined more by competition than cooperation. Several groups are left to fight and compete among themselves for funds and to protect their interests, rather than to work together for a common political goal. Even though the importance of creating coalitions among women groups should not be underestimated, this proves to not be sufficient to really challenge state policies and to ensure the political recognition of women. Women's power must be demonstrated through political activism, a locally grounded vision and a visible presence in the streets. As Fayza Abul Naga, minister for international cooperation and planning, recently noted, in order to "restore the role of women in Egypt towards democracy, women must take the lead in political parties and transitions" (Fayza Abul Naga's statement at UN Women Conference "Pathways for Women in Democratic Transition" in Deejay 2011). Indeed, despite the fact that women's membership in different coalitions and women groups has absolutely increased after the revolution, the type of women's organizations continued to be mainly feminist in orientation and composed by upper- and middle-class women who continue to address the "woman question" as a special case. Additionally, the stigma of having somehow been associated with Suzanne Mubarak's policies still remains a reason for the general social rejection of these groups. The failure of secular women to be taken into consideration is evident if compared to the activism of Islamist women, who, on the contrary, are mainly working for the cause of their parties in view of the coming elections. Secular feminism has been for too long rooted in the soil, but it has missed a widespread ideology and constituencies, while Islamic feminism has developed constituencies and a strong, well-received ideology. As a result, in order for women to be politically accepted, it will be fundamental to equate women's requests to the broader cause of social justice and democratization to avoid labeling women's demands as gender-driven. Only in doing so will women succeed in ensuring that gender issues will actually get translated into positive gender outcomes in the post-transition period.

CHAPTER IV

EGYPTIANS SPEAK: SOCIAL PERSPECTIVES ON WOMEN'S RIGHTS IN THE POLITICAL TRANSITION

The previous chapter described the effects of the recent Egyptian revolution on women's civil and political rights, and how the transitional government and main political forces are answering to women's call for greater participation in the country's political affairs. It can be concluded that although women's participation was remarkable during the revolution, in the transitional period, women have been put on the sidelines of the political scene. While some policies, like the quota, have been quickly removed, and women have been excluded from any official consultative process, their rights have also been endangered by conservative groups calling for the removal or amendment of the family laws. A fragmented women's movement, divided between secularists and Islamists and young and old generations, is arduously trying to merge in coalitions and unions in order to defend the status of women in the two main areas currently under attack: women's political roles and personal status rights. This has led to an increase in gendered social activism and civic participation, and to a proliferation of active women. Differently from the previous chapter, which introduced political events through an analysis based on experts' voices, this chapter will instead, mirror the arguments already touched upon in the previous section through a case study based on interviews, focus groups, and a survey, in order to report the opinions of ordinary Egyptians on the main events related to women's participation in the political transition.

In this chapter, the discussion will focus on the answers to the following questions: What do Egyptians think about the participation of women in the revolution? And how do they judge women's political exclusion from the current decision-making process? What kinds of feelings have the events of March 8 provoked among the average Egyptian? Are Egyptians socially and culturally prepared to recognize the role of women in high politics and the election of a woman as president? What do Egyptians think about feminism in general, women's groups specifically, and their current activism? How do Egyptians look at the political role of Islamic groups, their approach toward gender issues, and their attempt to amend the Personal Status Laws? The methodology used regarding the field work, research sample, and process of recruiting respondents was discussed in the first chapter. [61] Thus, at this point, the above questions will be addressed directly.

4.1 Results from the case study

With a combination of qualitative and quantitative research methods (open-ended questions, focus group discussions, and a survey), this case study allowed me to add real, concrete insights to the historical moment and political context of women's activism in Egypt. The scope of the semi-structured interviews has not been that of homogenizing the different kinds of respondents targeted, but offering an in-depth account of those movements involved in the process. In addition, four focus groups were held in order to explore in detail some of the issues elaborated upon individually during the interviews. An empirical study with this population of participants enabled me to draw conclusions about the common perceptions of women's political involvement in the revolution, consequences for women's rights, patterns of equality in family laws, and common perceptions of women's participation in positions of political leadership. Similar perceptions were also tested through an online questionnaire.

The data gathered from the interviews, focus groups, and the survey will be discussed in two parts. The first part will reflect the arguments that have been discussed in the previous chapter through a representation of the opinions of ordinary Egyptians. The second part will present, in a broad way, people's views on the main problems and difficulties women face in Egypt, as well as some ethnographic/personal observations on focus group participants' interactions.

4.1.1 Egyptians on women's participation in the revolution

Despite the different social backgrounds, levels of education, and political orientations of the participants in the case study, there were many similarities between their responses. University graduates, males and females, perhaps most enriched the debate.

Overall, the participation of women in the revolution has been positively and collectively accepted, seen as a sign of social unity for achieving a democratic change. For those who participated in this case study, the active role of women was a duty for some and an inspiration for others. From the survey sample, only a small percentage of the respondents—10.8 percent of males and 4.9 percent of females—think that political activism and street demonstrations are not appropriate for women.

For Amir, a physiotherapy student with liberal views and supporter of ElBaradei: *"Women have been a model for all; with their example, they pushed men to stay; they have been martyrs, mothers, and wives of the martyrs. This is how Egypt should always be."* For Farah, a student of law: *"Having women in the streets during revolutions is a very normal thing to happen. But I admit that for the typical Egyptian woman living under particular religious and cultural restrictions, this has been a real challenge. It was impressive to see many girls treated by the police officers in the same way men were treated."* And also for Mahmoud A., a young man with liberal orientations who participated in the first focus group, *"Women had an igniting role. Khaled Said's mother was one of the people who called for this revolution."* Khaled, a lawyer, views women's participation as a religious obligation when he says: *"Women were participating in wars in al Jahilia time (before Islam). This revolution was Jihad."*

Some participants also underlined how, with the end of the regime, women's political awareness has definitely increased. Some of those interviewed argued that women's political involvement changed after the revolution, and now, many young women have discovered a new interest in politics. For Fareeda A., a young woman and a supporter of ElBaradei: *"One of the great conquests that we have achieved through the revolution is the increased awareness of women about political stuff. Something changed inside women, also in those who have been following the events, only the TV."* But for the majority of the respondents, women's participation in street demonstrations should not be seen as an extraordinary achievement. Women's activism is judged by many as a normal struggle for a common cause, as women have suffered from the same social injustices as men and participated in the uprisings for the same reasons. This opinion is shared by 58.1 percent of male and 54.1 percent of female respondents to the survey, who believe that women's participation should be expected, as women represent half of society. For Mervat, a psychologist who lives in a poor suburb of Maadi: "*Women should participate because they are half of the society, and they went to the streets because social injustice was not for men only.*" For Salma, a secular writer and teacher and a self-declared anti-feminist: "*Women's participation should not be considered a separate outcome of the revolution. This is discrimination. There are no differences between women and men in first place. Their participation was equal, as gender has nothing to do with why people went to the streets.*"

For many of those who participated in the case study, the absence of sexual harassment in the streets, the infamous *tahrosh*, can be considered another positive achievement of the revolution. "*People were responsible and decent,*" confirms Adam, a TV director. This was also reported by 59 percent of females and 47.3 percent of males in the survey.

However, several participants reported common concerns over what is socially and religiously acceptable regarding the presence of women in the public sphere. Sleeping in Tahrir Square overnight and participating in the sit-in was not tolerable. For the average Egyptian, there are some social and gender norms prescribed to both men and women that cannot be taken too lightly. Doria, a general doctor, explains: "*It was too dangerous for women to be out during curfew without the protection of the male members of the family.*" And Zanati, a taxi driver, adds that: "*Religion does not allow women to be in dangerous situations and to sleep outside without husband and family. This goes against the dignity of the woman.*" Also for Imen, an engineering student who participated in the family focus group: "*It is not a problem if women want to go to the streets and demonstrate, but under the frame of* Shari'a. *She can go, but with men.*" [62] The same opinion is shared by all female participants in the family focus group. This underlines how in Middle Eastern patriarchal society, women are still requested to maintain honorable behaviors in all circumstances. As Botman also puts it, that means women should behave modestly, without talking, laughing, or acting energetically in public (Botman 1999, 108). For Farah, however, women's participation in sit-ins and night watches were a sign of new strength: *"Women, by participating in street demonstrations, have challenged many of the social traditions."*

Square: reflecting on March 8 *Tahrir* 4.1.2 Women and

Average Egyptians have generally condemned the assault on women who demonstrated in *Tahrir* Square on March 8. For many respondents, the revolution has given both women and men the right to express their public opinions. The new Egypt has released many forces, and all deserve their chance to speak. For many others, sexual harassment and violence have been, in past years, the signs of a wide-ranging sense of frustration and powerlessness among many young Egyptians. The blame goes to the corrupt regime and economic instability more than to the patriarchal roots of Egyptian society. For Doria: *"After the revolution, all people must use their chance to express their opinions, and women also must take their chance."*

However, for some others, this was not the right time and place for women to ask for isolated requests. Women are accused of having fragmented the demands of the revolution, having hijacked its cause, and having expressed their political demands in an aggressive way. For Salma, for example: *"Women deserved what happened to them. You cannot go to Tahrir Square and ask for women's rights a few weeks after the revolution. This was not the right time for that."* For Mervat: *"Women have not been 'diplomatic' in their requests; they were not supposed to go to the square immediately after the revolution."* The women's movement, she thinks, should focus on concrete actions instead of merely shouting and holding antagonistic banners. This shows that for many Egyptians, women's groups may sound hostile and risk sounding antagonistic to the rest of the society.

For other participants, what happened in *Tahrir* is still a clear sign of the unchanged patriarchal nature of the Egyptian society. For some, gender equality was preserved only in the eighteen days of the revolution; society indeed has not yet revolutionized its way of looking at women in the public sphere. Amir's feelings are clear: *"It was a catastrophic day. I was very depressed. Those are fanatics; they are infiltrators in our society and culture. Those cannot be the same youth that made the revolution."* Mohmena believes the same, considering the assaulters thugs who were probably paid by someone to create chaos and compromise the revolution. Also, for Fareeda A: *"Women's human rights were violated that day. Thus, I decided that I have to do something for women. Perhaps women need to have a cultural revolution."*

Also, the survey shows these divisions among the respondents: 34.8 percent considered that day the right time and *Tahrir* the right place for women to ask for their demands after the revolution. On the contrary, 35 percent opposed any kind of social division that might compromise common requests made during the transitional phase. Finally, 40.9 percent were disappointed and 33 percent were strongly disappointed about the events. This represents a clear sign of how Egyptians think and the hope they have for the post-revolution period to bring social acceptance and fraternity, which were the basis of the uprising's success.

4.1.3 Can women lead in Egypt? An analysis

In Egyptian history, several women have held leading positions; Queen Hatshepsut, Cleopatra, and Shajar al-Durr, sultana of Egypt in 1250, are some of the famous examples. In recent history, none of the Arab countries has had a female president, although queens, princesses, and first ladies have assumed outstanding political roles, such as Rania of Jordan, Princess Moza of Qatar, and Egyptian first ladies Jihan Sadat and Suzanne Mubarak.

The recent revolution, however, opened doors to new democratic aspirations and for women to participate in parliamentary and presidential elections. Bothaina Kamel is the first female candidate for the presidency in Egyptian history, and her candidacy has ignited public debate. However, the decisions to exclude women from the formation of the new Constitutional Committee and the ministries have alarmed those who believe that democracy cannot be achieved without sound gender equality. The opinions of those who participated in the focus groups and interviews are somewhat diverse, but they tend to be critical, for social, religious, and biological reasons, of the idea that women could lead in Egypt.

For Reem, for example: *"If no women were qualified to be part of the Constitutional Committee, why can't we accept this decision? Do we need to put women in, just for a question of décor? Besides, whoever takes any ministerial positions in this period is going to have big responsibilities. Women should think twice before struggling for these positions."* For many other respondents, the lack of women in the transitional government's process of consultations was not planned intentionally. For Ahmed B.: *"This cannot be considered a voluntary exclusion. I refuse the idea of an intentional exclusion of women. There is no persecution of women, but there is a request for qualifications."* This is also confirmed by 35.4 percent of survey respondents.

For some others, the blame goes to Egypt's patriarchal society and the scarce support for women in politics. For Somaya, a young female activist: *"Society and people do not support and help women who want to be active in public work; as a result, we do not have women in higher positions, and they do not have the motivation to go for a leading position. Before the old regime collapsed, women were not part of political life, and the same practice still exists. In my opinion, the revolution is still ongoing, we did not change anything but the president, the society is still the same and did not change much."* Leila, who participated in the same focus group but does not consider herself an activist, has very similar opinions: *"This is a patriarchy and a masculine society. You will always hear things like, 'This is not okay,' 'This is dangerous,' 'This is shame,' etc. It starts from the family, which most of the time does not support you."* Samy and Mohammed B., participants in the second focus group, argue the same. For Samy: *"The revolution did not change the mind of men. We didn't change all the worst that there was in the society."* And for Mohammed B.: *"From a very young age, women are taught that the most important thing is to get married, not to be politicians."* And for Farah: *"The empowerment of women shouldn't come only from the idea that we should have female ministers in the government. What we need are qualified people without any sexual differentiation. Unfortunately I think that the Egyptian woman is still not prepared to be a leader. The environment in which she has been raised made her a follower more than a leader. Measuring the success of a woman here is not about being a successful person in society or being a qualified worker, but by getting married and having children."*

A central issue to the debate also relates to the social roles that are genetically opportune to women. Participants resorted to the notion of *fitrah* (women's basic nature) to distinguish between permissible and forbidden occupations. The issue of the emotionality of women is a recurrent explanation for the incapability of a woman to lead. According to many participants, women, for physical and psychological reasons, are excluded from occupations that are considered appropriate for men. For Mervat, a psychologist: *"Women are definitely more sensitive. Their hormones are not stable all the time, like those of men. During the menstrual period, women might be impulsive and unfair while making decisions. In Western countries, however,"* she added, *"women have been taught to control their feelings. In the Middle East, women are still too sensitive."* Mervat, therefore, supports women working in ministries but not as presidents or prime ministers. And for Reem: *"Equality has limits; for example, I will not say that I want to be a petrol engineer and go live in the desert. This is something that I cannot deal with."* The same idea is also repeated by Khaled, who brings up the same example when he says: *"I do not agree with letting women work in whatever they want. It is mentioned in the Qur'an that God does not impose any person to do something that cannot be handled. Hence, a woman cannot do jobs that are too risky, like working in the field of petrol."* Of another opinion is Magdi, from the same focus group, who answers Khaled by saying: *"I don't agree with prohibiting women from doing the job they want. Let her do it and see how she deals with it."* Adam and Reem also raised another important point in relation to women's natural features. For Reem, leading a country could make women tired and compromise marital relations. *"These kinds of women do not take care of their families enough, and their well-being might be compromised."* *"Women are weak,"* explains Adam. *"They need to take care of husbands and kids. A woman is a leader in her home, but she is not supposed to take roles that are for men. Because women are working, many men are unemployed. God says that women's roles are to take care of their families first. Men can be losers too, but a good parliament will make a male leader stronger."* Or, as Fares says: *"Women could make wrong decisions that could comprise the entire country."* And Khaled, again, says: *"I do not prefer having women in administrative or political positions. Women are created out of a man's twisted rib. This rib is protecting the heart, and this is why women tend to be more emotional."* When we were discussing this issue, Mariam, a young liberal girl, reported the case of Cleopatra, who decided to leave the command of the army, thinking she was the reason for its failure because of her sensitivity. She also added: *"The current Egypt is not so different; men still think that giving power to women will be a disaster."*

Almost all women from the family focus group except for one, Menna, believe that women tend to be moody and might make wrong decisions during critical moments. For Imen: *"Women cannot control their minds."* For Abrar: *"God created two parts in human brains. Women have more patience than logic in their brains. For this, God gave men the chance to divorce, because men are capable of making rational decisions."* The above position suggests that the overall standpoint on gender roles, delineated according to biological differences, still continues to inform the vision of many Egyptians.

Turning toward political reasons, several respondents argue

about the necessity of coagulating forces around strong political leaders. For Salma: *"It is not the time to focus on this idea. The society will accept it when the way of thinking will be changed, and after having changed many other things in society, but not now."* As Egyptian history shows, women have always been asked to wait to push aside their own demands until the larger goal has been accomplished. It seems that "being a man" is considered a desirable characteristic by many voters, making it hard for a woman to get elected for this position.

For many participants in this field work, there is also a religious explanation for this. For Islam, a member of the Salafi group, explanations are based on the Islamic *Shari'a* and *fatwas*. *"In Islam, the majority of scholars agreed that women cannot take the position of Wilayah 'Ammah, or the presidency. Sheikh Saqr said that the majority of scholars did not agree on having women working as judges because of their biological features, which can affect their opinions and conditions. It is not allowed for women to participate in election battles in order to protect their femininity, dignity, and honor."* Islam also explained that the leadership of women is not recommended by religion. The basis for this assertion is that the Prophet Mohammed (PBUH) has, in a *hadith*, emphatically stated that any society which has its leadership under a woman will never succeed. He insists by saying: *"Manhood is a pre-condition for those who want to lead a country; woman is not, most of the time, prepared to take such a role. This does not lessen women's important role, which is that requested to them by nature and God."* For Khaled as well: *"Women can be the second man, but not the first. They can be consultants for the president but not presidents for the reasons that Islam mentions."* In the same focus group, Magdi seems to hold a different opinion. He believes that qualifications should represent the main criteria for taking any position, and not gender or religious ones. Besides, he argued that in the book of *Fiqh Al Dawla* by Sheikh Yusuf Al Qaradawi, it is explained how God created the *Ijtihad* in order to interpret the Qur'an and having different opinions in regards to the content of the religious sources. Hence, the above *hadith* can be contextualized, according to Magdi. Mahmoud B., from the same focus group, also believes that the *Wilayah 'Ammah* should be freely chosen by people, who might select a man or a woman. A similar discussion took place during the second focus group, where, according to Ahmed C., a president should be, first of all, physically strong. For Fareeda B. and Samy, however, working as a president only requires mental capacities and administrative skills. For Fareeda B., especially: *"Egyptian society still does not understand that we no longer live at the time of the Prophet, and what was not allowed before might be allowed in modern time."* With a more positive perspective, Zen believes that: *"Women can become presidents of the whole world; the importance is in the qualifications they have. I will personally be so happy if the new president is a woman, if she has all the qualifications for this position."* For those who support women's roles in politics, the only criterion seems to be in the qualifications women have to occupy the position. It seems indeed that the Mubarak regime, by electing women to Parliament under the umbrella of the NDP, has corroded people's trust toward women in politics. As Doria explains, *"People wanted to see a real change. The lack of women in the new government happened as a reaction to Suzanne Mubarak and the parliamentarian women members of the NDP."*

The respondents to the survey seem to have, on the contrary, a much more positive perspective. Thirty-three percent disagree and 48.2 percent strongly disagree with the idea that politics is a male-only field. In addition, 26.6 percent were disappointed to see a scarce representation of women in the transitional government, while 30.6 percent were neutral about this choice. Noteworthy also is the fact that 40.7 percent believe that with democratization, women's social roles will progress. However, almost 60 percent of male survey respondents still remained anchored to the idea that women cannot be president of the country, confirming that gender divisions persevere unchanged within popular mentality.[63]

4.1.4 Maintaining or abolishing the quota system in Parliament

At the time the research was conducted, there were speculations about a possible cancellation of the quota for women in Parliament. This was not made official by the Supreme Council of the Armed Forces (SCAF) until after the interview period had ended. However, overall, participants in this study were not particularly concerned about the abolishment of the quota for women, seen by many as discriminatory and unnecessary. It was frequently stated that women involved in political activities should demonstrate their capacities individually without waiting to be blessed by the "quota women." Many respondents think that women should now consolidate their efforts around other political gains, like participation in political parties, rather than asking for separate rights and in doing so, risking the revival of anti-feminist backlash. Adam argues: "*Women went to the streets during the revolution, demonstrating their power and political activism. They need to prove the same qualities in their political struggle without being helped through the quota.*" Ahmed A., Oracle developer, also adds: "*I am against the quota. If women want to be part of Parliament, they need to go through an equal competition. In my city, people voted for a woman for a long time* [he reported the case of Gamalat Rafae]. *Women are able to succeed without being pushed, and if men do not vote for them, they can search for the support of other women. But they need to have a program in order to assist women in the grassroots and women workers. I am sure that in this case, they will be supported and elected.*" For Reem: "*The quota is an insult to women's rights.*" For Salma as well: "*Why should women be considered special and different in this way? There is no need to put a specific number of seats in Parliament. I see that it is better for everyone to run for elections, and to let people free to choose the qualified ones, whether they are women or men. If a woman is successful, and qualified, they will vote for her, but we do not want to be forced to have women in politics just because of the quota."* For Islam, who works at the Ministry of Islamic *Wafd*, the idea of quota only exists in underdeveloped societies. However, he also stresses another point. For Islam: *"Democracy also means to be able to accept the idea that the new Parliament might be composed by men only. Everyone can run for elections—Muslims, women, Christians—but if the people choose all Muslim men, this selection should be collectively accepted."*

The focus group participants expressed similar opinions. For Mahmoud A.: *"The quota represents a particular kind of gender discrimination. It represents a patriarchal way of controlling women's presence in the political space. Women can take more than this."* For Fareeda A., Ahmed C. and Samy, those in Parliament should be only those who deserve the place, either men or women. Doria adds: *"In the past, this was tolerable because the role of women was marginal and there was a need for a quota. But now, there must be free and fair elections for all to be candidates, and people will choose who they want."*

Particularly, in the family focus group, a debate started between those who support women working in political positions and those who see women in Parliament as job stealers. This underlines how a part of Egyptian society still sees women as natural caretakers, not strong politicians.

Finally, Amir tackles another issue, saying: *"The quota is unfair. The quota was not made for the noble goal of making women reach leading positions, but it was made to increase the number of supporters of Mubarak's regime. I hope that the new people in the government will try to change the concept in the whole country, to bring women in the next parliament, just convincing people without forcing them. It must become an eternal right."* The transitional period is indeed showing how women are paying the price for choices made by the past regime. Having been the quota introduced unilaterally by President Mubarak, and having numerically strengthened the number of seats for the NDP, many Egyptians associate this with the old regime. There is a general inclination to cancel whatever initiative the regime government took. The resentment toward the former first lady, following accusations of her corruption, is another reason for this. In the elected Parliament of 2010, there were many complaints from women cadres and competencies on electoral fraud in favor of other less competent or less popular competitors (Abdel Hamid Hafez 2011).

On the contrary, for very few respondents, the quota system in Parliament represents an important provision in the current transition, which serves to achieve gender equality and give women the chance to prove their capacities. For some participants, Egyptian society is still extremely patriarchal and not yet ready to open the doors to the political engagement of women. Zen and Monir believe in the importance of having a fixed quota for women as a way of urging society to accept women in leading roles. In the future, with the installment of a democratic system, the quota will no longer be needed.

The survey results also show a similar perspective. Sixty-four percent of male respondents prefer to see women represented in Parliament based on their capacities and skills. Meanwhile, 34 percent of women support the quota, at least temporarily. Only a very tiny percentage supports the quota without hesitation, although men are overall more against this idea than women. Many respondents are still uncertain about the future role of women in politics, but they are confident that a new and democratic Egypt will recognize and highlight this fundamental equality.

4.1.5 A social reading of Egyptian feminist groups

For the average Egyptian, being a feminist or being part of a women's rights group is equivalent to standing for Suzanne Mubarak's cause. The erroneous association of the feminist movement with the National Council of Women (NCW) is reported on several occasions. It is clear that the predominant role of Mrs. Mubarak has somehow influenced the way the Egyptians look at women's issues. It is also important to note that the majority of respondents tend to generalize and merge NGOs' work with women's or feminist groups' activities. This is also due to the fact that the focus group and interview participants reported a certain ignorance on what exactly these groups or NGOs do, who they are, and what message they are trying to convey.

Many participants also have a problem with the term "feminism." It seems unacceptable in the current transition to have a separate women's movement instead of a cohesive, democratic social movement. Many of them are reluctant to distinguish between women's oppression and social oppression as a whole. They advocate that what was happening to women was happening to men, as part of a societal process in which human rights were either absent or morally bankrupt and corrupted by the regime (Karam 1998, 13). The rejection of feminism makes sense in light of the extreme reluctance to separate women's issues from those of the larger society. As Karam precisely explains, the term is also associated with stereotypes, like the fact that feminists are masculine, unreligious, and are calling for sexual promiscuity. The term feminism is impregnated with Western connotations and Orientalist superiority (Karam 1998, 6). For the average Egyptian, feminism is an ideology than cannot be fused with the Islamic one. As Amir explains, *"The feminist movement on the model of the Western one gives me a negative impression. Feminism with a Western matrix cannot be tolerated in Egypt. I am referring to when they talk about homosexual rights. This can't be understood in our society and culture."* And for Marien, *"Suzanne Mubarak destroyed the women's movement. I don't think that she really believed in what she was doing, but was only interested in maintaining her position."*

Others underlined the cultural lack of authenticity of feminist groups and their remoteness from the causes of common people. For Mariam, *"The movement is failing to address ordinary women. You can see that many women still don't know about their rights. I am speaking about the old tradition of feminists. But the new girls of the revolution represent a new and clean face, because they are asking for freedom and social justice for all."* Mervat instead has a more positive attitude when she explains, "*The exist-ence of women's NGOs is important for those who need assistance, and they deserve to be respected.*" However, she underlines, "*Not all are successful, and some of them have eccentric ideas. Sometimes it seems to me that they want to Americanize our society. So far, I didn't see any important achievement, except for the* khul'.*" As Ahmed B. also reiterates, "*I reject the fact that those women activists present Egyptian women as weak and oppressed. All society was oppressed before the revolution. They think themselves superior and developed; they see problems everywhere, whereas instead, simple women do not face all of this. I attended some of these meetings and found half of their words in English.*" Reem is also very direct in her critique when she says, "*Where are these activists when women really need them? My cleaning lady searched for the help of these groups when she was beaten by her husband, but no one helped her. These kinds of groups reach out only to women who are educated. They don't know what social justice means. They don't go to the low levels of society.*" Although Zen considers the newly formed women coalitions as an important achievement, he also thinks that, "*Women activ-ists are continuously choosing the wrong approach. People from the streets do not understand what they are talking about. Women's groups should speak in simple language if they want to reach simple people. Normal women do not care about the* khul' *when what they need is to have decent work and economic assistance. Common people are sometimes against these kinds of groups because they think that they could represent a threat to the stability of society. The mistake is on women's groups, who are not successful in explaining that their requests are for the achievement of basic human rights.*" And Salma: "*I am against having feminist activism. I don't believe that there should be a feminist movement, especially after the revo-lution, because the freedom that we are asking for is not for women or men only; it should be for the whole country. If the country re-covers its lost freedom, women won't need to ask for their specific rights anymore. Marriage and divorce problems are also not on the priority list. Women should only focus on the national struggle.*" Some participants also stress on the lack of religiosity of these groups, considered too secular and alien to society. For Fareeda A., *"They use an anti-Islamic language; they have to tone down the language they use with poor classes."* And for Islam, *"These groups should speak an Islamic language. Nawal El Saadawi wants children to be called after their mother's names and to abolish polygamy and virginity. They tend to have Western thinking, and this is exactly why I think that these organizations have failed."* As for women in the family focus group, opinions diverge. For Abrar: *"All these groups are losers, and they all encourage women to deviate from their home. And this is why the divorce rate is increasing."* And for Sara: *"The khul' had a very bad effect on the society. What they achieved with it was just to increase the problems in Egyptian families instead of resolving them."* Of a different opinion seem to be Asmae and Marwa, who consider the *khul'* an important achievement that these groups succeeded in obtaining.

Finally, some participants also underlined how the revolution has given voice to a new and young generation of politically active females; the hope seems to be centered on the new generations to propose a revised form of gender struggle. As Somaya argues, *"If we look at the new generations, we can see a new kind of feminism. These feminists are calling for freedom and social justice, but the old feminists still have their old traditions. If we succeed to direct the country toward a new road, this will affect all. The new feminists have another kind of feminism, a modern one."*

However, the majority of respondents to the survey maintain a critical opinion toward women's groups in Egypt—32.4 percent strongly agree and 39.6 percent agree that Egyptian women's groups have a Western agenda. In addition, 20.2 percent strongly agree, 34.2 percent agree, and 18.4 percent are neutral in considering these groups formed mostly by members of the upper class. Overall, women's groups continue to be discredited on the basis of their class affiliation and education, without considering their different ideological inclinations, activities, and specific contexts in which they operate.

4.1.6 Debating the Personal Status Laws: the *khul'*, the custody

law, and the legal age of marriage[64]

The public debate over the Personal Status Laws has been one of the most discussed trends of the transitional period. For eight months, newspapers, programs, and public debates, etc., have turned around laws that have been labeled as the "Suzanne Mubarak" laws. Conservative religious groups, such as Salafis, and others, like the "Save the Egyptian Family" association, have taken to the streets several times in the last few months, asking for the withdrawal of laws that they consider un-Islamic and discriminatory against men. The feminist movement has been repeatedly attacked for having pushed these laws ahead during the Suzanne Mubarak era, inevitably hampering the well-being of the Egyptian family.

Respondents to the focus groups, interviews, and survey have very different opinions and views about the Personal Status Laws. However, several participants felt they lack expertise and did not have much to say to questions related to the Personal Status Laws. This seems to confirm the fact that the average Egyptian does not perceive the debate over the Personal Status Laws as an urgent argument of discussion or their defense as a priority of the post-revolution transition. However, the issue of the *khul'* law, eleven years after its implementation, is still the topic that, more than the others, inflames the debate. Some of the respondents have different opinions on the correct interpretation and implementation of the law. For some, the *khul'* law as introduced under the direction of Suzanne Mubarak gave more rights to women that those stated in the prophetic *hadith*. For some respondents to the survey, a diverse interpretation of the *khul'* should be implemented according to which women can divorce themselves after previous consent from their husbands. For some, the current form of *khul'* takes away men's unilateral right to ask for divorce. Men indeed have been rationally granted the right to divorce, while women, being emotional beings, should have a much more limited access to it. For Islam, a participant in the third focus group, a lot of pressure from the women's movement and Suzanne Mubarak has been placed on Mohammed Said Tantawi, the previous *sheikh* of Al Azhar, to amend the law. For him, this was not the result of rational choice, but of political pressure. Some participants in the focus groups highlighted the increased rate of divorce after its introduction. Abrar and Sarah, members of the family focus group, showed the strongest refusal of the *khul'* citing its bad effects on society and Egyptian families. For both of them, the *khul'* gave women an easy way to escape from marital relations. A similar idea was reiterated by survey respondents. Some of them argued that because of the fact that women do not need to explain the reasons of divorce, *khul'* has been used easily and without reason by many women. Other female participants in the same family focus group seem to have another opinion. For Marwa, the *khul'* is a mercy that God gave women and is recognized by Islamic law.

Some survey respondents also believe that the *khul'* in its current form is still discriminatory, because it forces women to give up all their financial rights. One respondent says that the *khul'* is a relief from slavery, since women are requested to pay for their freedom. Also, for Zen and Mohmena, the Personal Status Laws remain deeply discriminatory against women, as they have been modeled according to men's views and needs. The statistics of the survey mirror the kind of answers reported so far, showing that 56.4 percent of men and 47.8 percent of women seem uncertain about which new shape the *khul'* should assume. Women are overall more in favor of the *khul'* (41.3 percent), while men are more against it.

As for reforming the custody law, the majority of respondents seem to be unified around the need of giving fathers more time with their children. However, also in this case, most of the participants seem to not really know what conservative groups are asking for. In their answers, participants refer to one side of the aspect, that of granting fathers more hours per week to spend with their kids, but they do not give clear opinions about the fact that the proposed reformed law will drastically reduce the age of custody of children to divorced mothers. Respondents to the survey argue that children suffer from psychological problems when separated for too long from their fathers. For others, the law is not compatible with *Shari'a,* as it gives mothers more time with their children and it is discriminatory against fathers. Doubts about the custody law seem to be even stronger among the respondents of the survey, with 72.2 percent of men and 61.4 percent of women saying that "they don't know" about the issue in question.

Finally, as for the idea proposed by some groups to reduce the age of marriage for girls from eighteen to sixteen, the majority seem to agree on maintaining the current law. However, some have argued that the Islamic *Shari'a* does not impose a precise age for marriage. For some survey respondents, sooner is better after the start of menstruation to avoid fornication. For others, this decision should not be up to the government and should remain a family issue. However, these can be seen as isolated answers, as the survey also shows that 78.3 percent of women and 67.3 percent of men agree in maintaining the legal age of marriage at eighteen years old.

4.1.7 Political Islam: perceptions of the Muslim Brothers and the Salafist movement

A total of 66.7 percent of men and 63.9 percent of women who filled out the survey consider themselves politically moderate. Only a tiny percentage openly says they are oriented toward political conservatism, and 61.8 percent of the total of male and 80.45 percent of female respondents call for the establishment of a civil state and for religion to be set apart from politics. Participants in focus groups and interviews were instead more politically varied. Initially, youth participants in the uprisings seem to be much more concerned and critical about the political activism of Islamic groups. Despite the fact that the Muslim Brotherhood should not be ideologically confused with the Salafi one, or with other associations, these are the two major movements around which the discussion has centered.[65] For some participants, religion-based political groups are the most dangerous threat for women's rights in Egypt because of their obsolete interpretation of religious texts and their manipulation.

Amir is very aggressive when he says: *"These groups are a bad model for our culture and religion. Egyptian culture and religion is for tolerance. People didn't die to see these extremists in power. They are like parasites. If they will take power, women will live like they are in Saudi Arabia."* Fareeda A. also underlines the lack of respect toward other religious creeds or political orientations. *"We cannot deny the role of the MB in the revolution, but now they are calling the liberal forces atheist. We need a culture of respect. They need to understand that this variety of ideas is useful. We need to have a civil Egypt for all Egyptians."* But she also stresses the political use and manipulation that these groups have of the woman question and social ignorance: *"The focus on women is to create instability; it has been always like this in the past. They used women's ignorance for their political goals."* And also, Fareeda B., a veiled girl and participant in the second focus group, says: *"Freedom of living and choice. I don't want to have someone that comes and tells me what I have to wear and do. The MB will put restrictions in place everywhere; they will make us live like at the time of Prophet Mohammed."* Also, Mariam believes that the religious groups are manipulating ignorant people to get their consensus: *"The MB participated in the demonstrations because they want to rule the country; they want to take all the political affairs in their hands. They have manipulated the ignorance of the people when they asked people to vote 'yes' during the referendum. They convinced people to vote for religion by voting 'yes'."* For Ahmed A., a political victory for these groups will undeniably have a negative effect on women's rights: *"If the Islamic groups take power, this will have a bad effect on to the entire society but especially to women."* The fact that conservatism might worsen women's conditions is also reiterated by Zen: *"They want women to stay at home, to be forced to wear the hijab and to abolish laws like the khul' because this was done at the* time of Suzanne Mubarak." And Mahmoud A.: "*The Salafists are the real danger for the revolution, for women, and society. They want to establish parties that prevent women from participating and call for forbidding them from being president.*" Many others simply do not trust conservative political groups, believing that they will never succeed in maintaining power. In this regard, Mohmena says: "*I do not trust them, and I am sure that they will not win. It has always been like this throughout history. They have been making agreements with the government, and then they have lost everything.*" And Salma: "*They are not religious. You are free to pray and fast, but you don't have the right to force it on society. The same goes for women's issues; they can't force women to do and to be what they don't want to do.*" Overall, the majority of the participants that I spoke to seemed to be sincerely concerned about the future political shape of the country; most of all, participants are worried about the effects of a lasting military control and/or Islamic authority.

Very few participants have openly stated their support for the cause of Islamist groups. Islam, for example, upholds that: "*The Islamists will support women's rights more than any other movement. The new Islamists are civilized and educated, and I think that such type of people will support women even more.*" Also, Marwa, a participant in the family focus group, argues: "*They will try to satisfy women. The Muslim Brothers support women; the proof is in the fact that they started to have female candidates. They will give more rights to women than in the past because they will give them what God gave, and women will have more dignity and pride than in the past.*" The same ideas are also shared by Abrar, who believes that conservative groups now more than in the past will be able to direct society toward a religious renaissance.

4.2 Addressing women's social difficulties and their causes

This section is mainly constructed around data collected from the open questions put forth in the survey. Even though the amount of data is enormous and the answers challenging, for space reasons, answers will not be deeply articulated but only reported without extensive explanations.[66] The responses given mainly focused on traditions, poverty, sexual harassment, women's reproductive health, and the impact of religious forces. A majority of the participants think that the major problem women face stems from the cultural attitudes and traditions. It became clear throughout the case study that conservative religious visions and patriarchy can be seen by both males and females as major reasons for women's social inequality. Biased interpretations of Islamic texts have been mentioned in particular as source of gender discrimination in Egyptian society. It is worth noting that in the survey, this was mainly reported by male respondents who underlined the risks associated with a masculine culture and a reactionary interpretation of religion. Women have given a much more practical rationale to gender inequality, highlighting documented facts, like economic disparities, political corruption, and lack of education. Some of the responses are here reported, as follows: *"Masculine customs and traditions too often harm women, forbidding them equal rights in all matters of life, like employment, family inequality, and social participation,"* or, *"women are socially treated as inferior and less capable than men, thus facing social, political, and economic inequalities,"* and, *"Egyptian society is male-dominated and women are seen as incapable of doing any real work. They make her feel that her place is at home and that she is not capable enough of doing anything independently."*

Some respondents have especially stressed domestic discrimination and different social roles transmitted to boys and girls. According to some, women internalize their subordinated position and their slavish nature. This is especially transmitted from generation to generation and from mothers to daughters. This is particularly correct in a country where 49 percent of young girls believe that they should obey their brother, even if he is younger (Population Council 21, 2010). This evidence is further supported by knowledge of genderized attitudes that are being inculcated in young boys and girls, whether by parents, school and/or the media. Some others have also written about social stigma suffered by divorced women or unmarried older women as another widespread source of suffering and frustration among women. Sexual harassment and insecurity in the streets are also frequently reported. Education is also reported by almost all participants as many Egyptians still see the lack of female literacy (especially in the rural areas) as one of the reasons for women's subordinate position. Amir argues in this regard: *"In some tribal areas, the illiteracy is 87 percent; this will not only make women unable to continue their education, but also to vote in the next elections."* And Mervat: *"Our society prefers men over women. If you don't have money, you prefer to send the boy to school and to keep your daughter at home. And I know that this also happens in Cairo."*

A number of interrelated issues also came up as cases of social instability. First of all, the economic stagnancy and unemployment rates tend to damage women more than men, as employers have a propensity to hire men, even in cases of parity in expertise. Hence, lack of employment forces many women to renounce a public social life and to deal exclusively with the roles of caretaker and housewife. As someone reported, unemployment is detrimental for men, escalating in sexual harassment in the streets and illegal marriages. In particular, the prolonged "waithood," with delays in family formation and setting up independent households, has been reported as one big cause for social problems. They wait in long periods of unemployment, living with parents, and are unable to pursue marriage or home ownership. And as it is harder for younger men to find opportunities, there are very few opportunities for young women to have an active voice in public life. There is absence of an enabling political, social, and economic environment for the participation of youth. The government is particularly blamed for not having established any welfare system and social protection for widows and divorced women. Media are also held responsible for portraying women as sexual objects and encouraging this behavior, and for being gender-blind. Finally, a discriminatory justice system and unfair family laws are seen by a few respondents as reasons for gender discrimination. However, only a handful of answers consider these laws a major problem, while many see corruption and economic injustice as the main cause for gender-related social problems. Lastly, some also blame women's groups for not being capable of creating strong organizations, and for basically not taking concrete steps toward the improvement of women's conditions.

4.3 Quick notes on personal observations of the focus group discussions

This work did not intend to follow the participant observation approach as a methodology while collecting data. However, the need to write a paragraph on "personal observations" came from the enriching personal experience I had while doing field work. Having targeted several kinds of Egyptians with differing social and political backgrounds, I could not avoid reporting some of the ethnographic observations that I have gathered while doing this study.[67] Indeed, "Participant observation is a qualitative method with roots in traditional ethnographic research, whose objective is to help researchers learn the perspectives held by study populations" (Family Health International 13). Through participant observation, it is possible to go beyond the simple analysis of written data, trying to learn more about the lives of participants; it is also useful to understand the relations among people, as well as among those in the same focus group. Simply, what is learned from this observation can help not only to study data collected through other methods, but also to deepen the analysis in order to have a better understanding of the phenomena that have been studied (Ibid., 14). During the focus groups, but also in the interviews, I have noticed many particular features in the sample of participants that I have targeted that, however, cannot be reported completely. However, in particular, the female-male interactions developed during the focus groups among participants have been noteworthy.

In the first focus group, there was an egalitarian division between the two genders, and the debate was equally interestingly articulated. The two female participants have exquisitely complemented each other. Somaya, in jeans and a tiny T-shirt, who considers herself an activist, almost never sits, speaking while standing and arguing animatedly. Leila, with a colorful veil and a long dress, entered the discussion after the first somehow brought into the discussion because of Somaya's charisma. Although the two women seem apparently from two different worlds, they have somehow influenced each other. Leila especially drew inspiration from the strength of the first, taking the courage to participate strongly in the debate. The third girl instead was almost silent, nodding encouragingly to what the other girls were saying. As for the two men involved, while one found the support of the girls, standing for the cause of women, the second one was repeatedly attacked for his conservative and sometime odd visions of women's roles and rights. Sometimes, the girls were successful in intimidating him and making him reason about his non-gender-friendly declarations. This focus group was perhaps a perfect combination of power relations between males and females in which females were able to dominate because of their charisma and speech articulation.

In the second focus group, there was much group consent. Being the members of the focus group, all youth, fresh graduates with the same level of education, their visions tend to complement each other and to be on the same wave of length. Also, the social background (low-middle class) and the political orientation (liberal) have been almost the same among participants. There were horizontal and peer-to-peer relations in the group, where, however, one voice—also in this case, the voice of a girl, Fareeda B.—stunned the other participants. She was particularly active in working as the main leader of the conversation and able on several occasions to bring the rest of the group to her side and vision of the story. Also in this case, a young girl dominated the debate and demonstrated an incomparable and strong personality. A case apart was the third focus group, where only men were involved. In this case, I noticed how women's absence led male participants to be much stronger and critical in their argumentations on the issue. This was not the case in the first two focus groups, in which I felt that men were occasionally retaining their feelings. But also in the third one, the imam, Islam, who came to the focus group wearing *ghalabya* and *takeyya,* was undoubtedly the leader of the conversation, thanks to his religious acquaintance. However, the other participants, with perhaps more liberal perspectives, were able to somehow counter-balance the argument. This was perhaps the most enriching focus group, in which I felt that gender unity gave participants free space for argumentation and liberation of ideas.

As for the family focus group, I regret to not have more space to report the large amount of ethnographic observations I collected during the forty minutes of debate. While I was invited to a Thursday gathering in one lower-class suburb of Maadi with my husband's acquaintances, I took the chance to initiate the focus group. Women and men were sitting in two different rooms, and women were able to talk openly. However, and although I was not a stranger to them, there was some delay to enter into the debate and fear of being reported. After I explained several times the confidentiality of the study, they felt released and their answers became animated. The aspect that mostly grasped my attention was the different thoughts that women from the same family were able to voice. Their arguments were indeed swinging from liberal to conservative to pro-Islamist. The intergenerational division was also stimulating, with the younger participants more emancipated and active and the older ones strictly conforming to gendered social norms. This enriching experience has also shown that when stimulated through horizontal and friendly researcher-researched or peer-to-peer communication, socio-economic differences and political divergences do not represent an obstacle in creating an egalitarian dialogue among women of different social classes and/or religious views. Many women are already energetic and empowered. It rests to see if and how this inspiring force will be stimulated by the new and old women's groups and political actors, using perhaps the logic of "paying attention" to what women really want more than simply arguing about gender submission on their behalf.

4.4 Sub-conclusion
Data of the case-study suggest that despite social, economic and political differences, the majority of the Egyptians have positively welcomed the participation of women in the past revolution. However, it has been analyzed how, in the current transition, Egyptians do not want to think in male-versus female-gendered blocks, looking at social justice and democracy as common goals that society is aiming to achieve as a whole. However, it is worth noting how, for the average Egyptian, women are seen as powerful agents of change and equal partners only and exclusively in some circumstances. While their participation in street demonstrations is considered remarkable in periods of change, leading political roles are still seen as inappropriate for women. Many believe that for biological and religious reasons, women are not suitable for practicing politics. Participants resorted to the notion of *fitrah* (women's basic nature) to distinguish between permissible and forbidden occupations. "Being a man" is considered a desirable characteristic for a president because he is considered not to be moody, weak, and irrational, as women have been frequently described. Interestingly enough, these visions are shared by both men and women, showing how patriarchy and hegemonic masculine visions of power have soaked the minds of both genders alike. Patriarchism has been polished in the eighteen days of the revolution, but the society has not yet revolutionized its way of looking at women in the public sphere. Egyptians however, seem to deny the evident patriarchism and masculinity of Egyptian society, pointing at economic and social instability as the main reasons of women's problems.
As for the "women quota" it was attacked by participants on the

grounds that it's an introduction of the previous regime, used for its own goals and not for empowering women politically and secondly with the argument that women should compete in the elections on their own merit and qualities without the help of a quota for women. Beyond a general unawareness about the importance of the quota system to achieve gender equality at political level, this was also the reflection of the fear of defending something so closely associated with the previous regime. It is clear that the predominant role of Mrs. Mubarak has influenced the way the Egyptians look at women's issues. For the average Egyptian, being a feminist or being part of a women's rights group is equivalent to standing for Suzanne Mubarak's cause. The cultural lack of authenticity of feminist groups, secularism and remoteness from the causes of common people are sufficient reasons to refuse the movement as a whole; the elitism of the movement seems to be the main reason for its refusal and the proof of its failure in achieving social justice among women. As Graham-Brown says, for Egyptian women to be free, they must "find an identity of their own—not only separate from men, but also challenging the negative view of their culture and society which is a legacy of colonialism and imperialism" (Graham-Brown 1981, 27).Noteworthy is the overspread unawareness of both men and women about the Personal Status Laws and women's rights under the law. This confirms the tendency that for, normal Egyptians, issues like divorce and child custody are not daily priorities and therefore are not investigated and prioritized. Furthermore, groups like the Muslim Brothers or the Salafis are not trusted, and secularism seems to be the political ideology that Egyptians want concretely put into practice.[68] However, for the majority of the Egyptians who participated in this research, religion still has a prominent role in their lives, seen as the pillar around which all social interactions turn.

V
CONCLUDING ANALYSIS

This research has examined the participation of women in the January 25 revolution as well as the development of women's political roles and rights in the transitional period. The work aimed to emphasize the power game played between the Egyptian state and women's groups at the time of the three presidents and in the current post-Mubarak period, investigating to what extent, in its transition toward democracy, the Egyptian state is willing to include women in national politics, and how women's groups are mobilizing in order to challenge the state's hegemonic discourse and thus succeed in improving women's political representation. Furthermore, through a study of the perceptions held by ordinary Egyptians, with regard to themes related to women's political rights, this work has also underlined how the participation of women in the revolution has affected the way Egyptians experience and consider the position of women in politics according to their social and religious perspectives.

5.1 Feminist activism and its impasse: reasons and lessons learned

In the aftermath of the January 25 revolution and after having assisted with the participation of women in protest marches, the topic of the relation between state politics and gender became extremely relevant in order to understand how women will be included in transitional politics and in the democratic discourse of the state. By looking at the development of feminism in Egypt and its relations with both the state and society, the first conclusion of this work is that, during the century, women's groups have not succeeded in counter-reacting effectively to the hegemonic power of the state and to a certain patriarchal discourse through powerful socio-political actions. Hence, this break-down is having repercussions on how the post-Mubarak state is engaging in gender politics, and how society looks at feminist activism and views women's political participation.

The work has shown how women's involvement in revolutionary struggles is not a new phenomenon. Women in Egypt participated in the battle against British colonialism in the early 1920s, fighting alongside men for a common nationalist cause. Women, however, were not able to convince male politicians to include their civil and political rights in the secular legislation and policies of the state, becoming consequently involved in a parallel public sphere at the margins of masculine political life (Botman 1999, 28; Badran 1996; Mariscotti 2008, 38). Until the 1950s, women's political representation had been feeble, and activists had consequently become involved in the feminist battle of the Egyptian Feminist Union (EFU).

During the century, there has been an enduring academic debate about feminist groups' ideology and identity. Several studies reported how their affiliation with Western values and their social backgrounds have inflamed the discussion over their local and cultural identities (Mariscotti 2008, Ahmed 1993, Botman 1999, Karam 1998). In a period during which Egypt was rediscovering its Islamic identity after years of colonialism, any identification with Western discourses and a Western-styled emancipation of women was seen as interference. In the period of nation-building, secular-feminist-activism evoked mistrust about its place within the local landscape of "traditions and authenticity" (Al-Ali 2000, 2). Besides, feminist activism became limited to a certain sector of society, and the impression was that those who were calling for political rights were only secular women, not representatives of the majority of the female population. According to some scholars, the struggle of the movement for issues like Personal Status Laws, such as those relating to polygamy and divorce, proved to not be a priority for women of the lower class, who did not benefit equally from feminist arguments (Mariscotti 2008, 1). Therefore, the representation of feminist groups as agents of a foreign agenda was intentionally and strategically used and abused by the state in order to discredit women's activism according to its plans, disregarding the nationalist and patriotic spirit of many of these women and their support for the cause of the Arab women.

Indeed, chapter two has shown how the state has continuously played out a power struggle with women's groups to both maintain and gain political authority and hegemony. By making a conscious use of tradition and religion, the state has used Islam as a means to reach its ends in terms of consolidating its ideological hegemony (Karam 1998, 23). The subordination of women in family's issues served to justify the state discourse, using Islam and social conservatism as proof of cultural authenticity, which helped legitimize the state with "traditional" sectors of society (Warrick 2009, 51). The Egyptian state has exercised political control over religious forces by retaining patriarchal forms of power over women; it is from this patriarchal dimension that feminists have tried to emerge and rebel (Badran 2009, 18). The challenge has been that of seeking alternative discourses of empowerment while simultaneously combating their subordination to the state and certain conservative religious groups (Karam 1998, 24).

Under Nasser and Sadat, contrasting measures were introduced to both include and exclude women to the general scheme of modernization and national development, making sure to frame women's liberties within state power. Power was clearly exerted on women in the field of the Personal Status Laws. To avoid any kind of political dissent with the Islamists and to maintain intact the religious legitimacy of the state, Personal Status Laws remained the point of balanced relations between these two forces. By granting women few rights in the field of the Personal Status Laws, the government demonstrated its ability to respect some of its international obligations without displacing religious laws altogether in order to pursue its partly traditionalist and partly liberal legitimacy (Moussa, 2; Warrick 2009, 4). Therefore, Egypt's case can be located under Connell's categorization of gender regimes, those in which the state is the central institutionalization of gendered power. As Connell puts it, "The state's power to regulate and shape gender relations can work toward the consolidation of existing gender relations, but it also has the potential to unsettle the existing gender order through reforms" (Connell, 1990 in Al-Ali 2002, 18-19).

Chapter two also showed how the feminist movement failed to constitute a successful political contender to the state under both Presidents Nasser and Sadat. As Warrick explains, the movement did not pursue any significant public and political change: "Change usually requires that women pursue social and political change, and that change is of a significant kind, usually requiring a restructuring of political and legal rights and implying expansion of both political participation and the nature of issues within the political arena. There is no feminist movement that constituted a direct opponent to state hegemony and a traditionalist discourse. Resistance must be carried out in local struggles against the many forms of power exercised at the everyday level of social relations" (Warrick 2009, 31-32). Without strategic alliances with powerful political and civil constituencies, the commitment of women's groups to redefining gender roles remained marginal; the little cooperation and coordination to face the state as one coordinated and strong front made the counter-reaction minimal.[69]

Unlike the Egyptian case, this work has indeed shown how the South African struggle against apartheid and the following democratic transition resulted in a major political role guaranteed to women, and their inclusion in the representative government, constitutional drafting, and policymaking process (Hassim 2002, 693). In South Africa, women activists consolidated themselves in one unique, independent, and organized political coalition, the Women's National Coalition (WNC), which was successful in introducing the notion of gender equality within the African National Congress (ANC) (Ibid., 694). As Hassim argues, "The existence of a strong political party that favored a structural transformation rather than merely a transfer of power and that, as a result of a slow process of internal transformation of decision-making processes and representational structures, had committed itself to eradicating gender inequalities, was a crucial factor" (Ibid., 696). Furthermore, the WNC represented a wide variety of women; it had good organizational capacity and facilitated a triple alliance of key women activists, academics and politicians of all races (Hassim, 2006 in Waylen 2010, 340).

Also in Chile, women, by enlarging their constituencies and creating alliances with political parties, succeeded in making their claims within the state and society mainstream. A number of independent feminists and women from political parties formed an alliance—the women's *Concertación de la Mujeres por la Democracia,* established in 1988 (Waylen 2010, 339). Thanks to this combined effort, *Concertación* became a successful tool for demanding women's rights in the new electoral process (Waylen 2007, 76). Women's groups succeeded in pushing for gender equality more within the frame of political participation than ideological separation while maintaining a strong social dimension (Ibid., 102). As both Hassim and Waylen have underlined, in South Africa and Chile, positive political opportunities and successful strategies adopted by women's groups have been crucial in differentiating the gender outcomes of these countries from those of Algeria, Morocco, Iran, and Egypt. In Egypt itself, not only have women's interests remained subordinated to state interests, but women's groups themselves have remained anchored to a sort of class elitism and often are incapable of creating larger constituencies and durable political alliances. Furthermore, they also have failed to link poor women's needs and interests with middle-class women's interests (Waylen 1994).

Chapter two has concluded its analysis by also looking at the controversial relations of some women's groups and NGOs with the first lady of Egypt, and the recent dispersion of feminist activism through civil society organizations. As Margot Badran has clearly explained, this "de-centered feminism is being expressed in the context of a massive proliferation of NGOs and at a moment when the pragmatic takes precedence over the ideological" (Badran 2000). Women's NGOs represent the development of an Arab civil society and a sign of a bottom-up democratic approach, but their dependency on foreign funds, as well as their ability to actually achieve social justice and development, created a debate about their identity and ideology (Jad 2004). The debate over "foreign funding" opened a resilient problem between the West and the Arab world. For several observers, the West is a menace for the identity of the Arab populations and the religion of Islam, and those that accept funds from abroad are considered to be aiding the economic exploitation or domination of Egypt by the West (Pratt 2001, 10). In the last years, foreign funding proved, however, to be necessary for the NGOs in order to operate due to the lack of governmental or other national sources of funding. While in Western countries, a part of state budget is allocated to civil society, in Egypt neither businesspeople (often linked to the regime) nor ordinary citizens have financed the activities of the NGOs (Ibid., 6).

But according to Jad, the main problem remains in the nature of civil society organizations, in their planning character, the social "targeting" limited by the time frame of the project, the competitiveness of their leaders, and the communication methods used—workshops and conferences—to "educate" people, which made the mission of women's NGOs not based on a common development goal, but more project- and business-oriented. Therefore, the potential to create substantial change through projects became fairly small, and human contacts, as well as personal-level communication with the constituencies, remained quite limited (Jad 2004). As a result, in recent years, Egyptian women's NGOs have failed to symbolize authentic mobilizing agents of social change and to concretely expand their constituencies. Women's groups and NGOs should now realize what they have never been able to achieve in several decades, such as expanding their social constituencies beyond the petty bourgeois which characterizes their ranks, by targeting women from the working and lower classes, and by actively supporting their demands of employment, education, and dignity. The transformation of these groups in one united, genuine movement will not be possible without being recognized and legitimized at the local and national levels from these lower social classes. In order to succeed in its requests for real gender equality, the movement should be based on the same cultural beliefs of the masses, and locally grounded with a vision through which social relations are organized (Tarrow in Jad 2004). It seems that the formula of women-activism-NGOization should find other ways of engagement with a local, grounded vision along class and religious lines, and a more sustainable power basis for gender/social justice change. Only in doing so will women succeed in making sure that gender issues will actually be translated into positive gender outcomes in the post-transition period. From now on, the real challenge for women's rights organizations will be that of reassessing their programs and approaches and becoming more mass-based, focusing on understanding what the Egyptian women really want, whether they agree with their political opinions or not.

5.2 After January 25: which revolution for women?
Chapter three has reported and explained in a sequential order the events that happened after the January 25 revolution. The factor that, more than others, has attracted the attention of international media has been the participation of women alongside men in marches of protest, slogans, braving tear gas, and blogging. As in 1919, women took to the streets for the same cause proposed by men; this time, they wanted to overturn the regime of Hosni Mubarak. The work went through the events of Tahrir Square by reporting the direct observations of both male and female activists involved in the revolution-

ary protests, as well as reporting the comments of ordinary Egyptians. The leading role played by women in the protests has been of utmost importance. The participation of women in the revolution has been positively and collectively accepted by those interviewed for this study, and seen as a sign of social unity for achieving democratic change. However, as many Egyptians have reported, women's active role in the streets was not exceptional but, on the contrary, expected. For the average Egyptian, women's participation in political protests should not be seen as an extraordinary achievement, but more as an ordinary social duty.

Chapter three has underlined how, after having drawn the curtain over Tahrir Square, the post-revolution period in Egypt did not maintain the promised ideal of equality and representation, instead worsening the binomial women-politics relation. As in the 1920s, a familiar political pattern made the dreams of the revolution unrealizable. Once competitive politics started to re-establish activities, thanks to the new political opening, for women, participation in national liberation did not guarantee an equal role in the outcome. The lack of women on the committee charged with amending Egypt's constitution, as well as their exclusion from any consultation process, the lack of female representation in the ministries, the gender-blindness of the party system, and the victory of conservative religious groups in the elections, cast doubt over whether the country can develop into a true democracy. Relentless cultural conservatism and patriarchal mentality proved to have been resistant to the revolution, as the events of March 8 and March 9 (when a group of women was violently subjected to virginity tests) demonstrated.[70] The harassment of women on International Women's Day proved that it will take much more time for women to prevail to the deep-seated misogyny of the male Egyptian population. During the protests, the participation of women was desired to the extent that women would advocate for the national cause, which in turn implied collective consciousness rather than individual gender-based requests. When women are no longer needed, however, the gender agenda is downgraded to the lowest priority level, and women making requests are seen as hijackers. While those who participated in this research have condemned the violence of the March 8 as an unjustified act of aggression, for the majority of the Egyptians, women's groups are still seen as suspicious. In the transitional period, secular women's groups have been seen as hostile, somehow aggressive in their requests, and detached from demanding a universal democratic process that would enable them to unify the efforts with those of the rest of the society.

The rejection of feminist groups by the Egyptians interviewed in this work makes sense in light of the extreme reluctance to separate women's issues from those of the whole society and women's groups' lack of broader social relations across class and religious lines. For the average Egyptian, feminism is an ideology impregnated with Western-influenced ideas than cannot be fused with the Islamic one. Furthermore, being a feminist or being part of a women's rights group is still equivalent to standing for the old regime in the person of Suzanne Mubarak who was involved in several women's rights activities through the National Council of Women (NCW). It is clear that the predominant role of Mrs. Mubarak in the amendment and introduction of laws concerning women's status has influenced the way the Egyptians look at women's issues. The introduction of reforms in the Personal Status Laws was very similar to the introduction of many other laws, in a top-down manner, leading to an incorrect association between a deeply heated regime and women's rights. As Dawood adds, "the state—and its associates—decided which women's rights were to be addressed as well as when and how they would be addressed, with Egyptian society almost entirely removed from this process. This led many people to feel that changes in women's rights were being imposed onto society" (Dawood 2011).

Therefore, in order to combat what seemed to be a retreat of women's rights, independent activists as well as women's NGOs mobilized and created coalitions to support the cause of women and their equal participation in the political process. However, there has been a lack of collective and tangible support for female parliamentary candidates and a numerically strong and visible engagement in Tahrir Square during the many phases of the revival of the revolution. Besides, as some experts interviewed for this work have also reported in chapter three, the relationship between groups and/or women's NGOs continues to be defined more by competition than cooperation. Groups are left to fight and compete for funds and protect their interests, rather than to work together toward a common goal. Indeed, the contemporary secular women's movement is still extremely diversified in terms of activities, structures, and institutional frameworks. NGOs with clear decision-making bodies exist side by side, with other less institutionalized groups. If some women are independently involved in political parties and/or human rights centers, others are walking independently and affiliate themselves with specific lobbying groups. Most of them have in common the fact of belonging to the same social classes, and even though the majority of them refuse conservative Islamist tendencies and discourses, among them divisions linger on how to approach the growing religiosity of the country (Al-Ali 2002, 14). Moreover, divisions among the old and new generations, as well as rivalry in terms of ideological and political truths, remain an obstacle to women-led political collective action, causing the movement to fail in sustaining adequate momentum (Ibid., 17). Indeed, as Tadros explains, any feminist movement, in order to be successful in strengthening women's collective action, should be able to negotiate the following relations: 1) reconciling autonomy with political integration; 2) building a constituency and developing broad-based alliances; 3) self-representation; and 4) internal inclusiveness. [71] Still, this work argues how feminist groups and women's NGOs are still failing to unite with a common political and ideological agenda and a movement discourse, as well as to build durable constituencies and develop broad-based polit-

147

ical alliances with the liberal forces engaging in politics. Moreover, foreign funding, especially in the coming period, will need to diversify its beneficiaries avoiding corrupting and fracturing the already bourgeoning Egyptian civil society. Funding, in order to lessen competition and assure sustainability, should be directed to women NGOs that have been allied organically with an unambiguous social and development agenda rather than to isolated groups and demands.

Concluding, Hassim clearly states how transition to democracy does not necessarily enhance women's political rights."Transitional periods and democratization can benefit women only to the extent that they are capable - both ideologically and organizationally - of mobilizing around their particular concerns" (Hassim 2002, 697).

5.3 The unchanged nature of Egyptian society

An unchanged reality, one that has not been tarnished at all by the revolution, is the prominent role that religion still has within Egyptian society and how it affects people's visions on women's rights. The empirical study proposed in this work has presented this sort of puzzling reality. Indeed, despite the fact that the majority of the participants consider themselves politically moderate, cultural conservatism and patriarchy remain rooted and hidden within society, among both women and men.

The images of public religiosity in Tahrir Square, with Islamic symbolism and various religious slogans, have underlined the role religion had in fueling and engineering the revolution, a trend that will, without a doubt, continue to propagate in the future (Abou El Fadl 2011, 312). In the last years, Islam has become the central feature of almost any discourse involving political, social, cultural, and economic change, and the Egyptian population, especially when considering the results of the recent elections, seems eager to include religion in the state politics in the coming period. This work has therefore highlighted how, despite social, economic, and political differences, the majority of the Egyptians targeted in this work are still anchored to patriarchal interpretations of what concerns women's roles in the public and political sphere.

Women participated in the revolution in substantial numbers, and both men and women protested and celebrated together in mixed-gender settings. Their participation was welcomed, respected, and seen as a sign of a growing social consciousness and normal civil duty. The gender dynamics and practices observed in Tahrir Square, as well as the free mixing of sexes, gave the impression of social freedom and a new role for women in the public space (Ibid., 314). However, as this work shows, common concerns remain over what is socially and religiously acceptable regarding the presence of women in the public sphere; specific gender norms prescribed to both men and women cannot be taken too lightly and cannot be overcome. In the Middle Eastern patriarchal society, women are still requested to preserve honorable behavior while in public. Thus, a respectable woman seems to be one who does not sleep in the square without the presence of a related man; she is also one that does not scream in public and does not take part in fighting.

Besides, leading political roles are still seen as inappropriate for women, and their inferior position is seen as justified for social, religious, and biological reasons. The opinions of those who participated in the focus groups and interviews are somewhat diverse, but they tend to be critical of the idea that women could govern in Egypt. Several participants resorted to the notion of *fitrah* (women's basic nature) to distinguish between permissible and forbidden occupations for women. The emotionality of women and their physical and mental inferiority are recurrent explanations for their inability to engage in political activities. Manhood is a pre-condition for those who want to lead a country; women are not, most of the time, prepared to take such a role. Women who aspire to leading positions rob the positions of men, as some of those interviewed have argued. However, this does not diminish women's important role, which is principally that of caretaker. Political roles are prescribed by religion to men, and women should avoid asking for a place in positions in which they would be considered inadequate, and instead focus their efforts as mothers and wives. In explaining this gender division of roles, some participants have relied on the religion of Islam, according to which both genders are complementary because each one has a pre-destined task that, if altered, might lead to social corruption.

It has been also remarkable to notice how these social visions are spread more among women than men. Many women interviewed consider themselves unable to control their minds and make rational decisions, having less logical reasoning. Allusions to the *Qur'an* and its interpretations have been frequent during the field work in order to justify these views. Several Egyptians claim that both the holy *Qur'an* and *hadiths* forbid women's access to political leadership, as clearly stated in Al Bukhari, wherein a society that has appointed a woman as a ruler will not thrive. Therefore, patriarchal thought, institutions, and behaviors largely remained resistant over time to the revolutionary *Qur'anic* notion of gender equality; the above position suggests that the overall standpoint on gender roles, delineated according to biological differences, still continues to inform the vision of many Egyptians.

Furthermore, beyond these religious-led visions, there is also an overspread lack of confidence for what concerns women's political qualifications in Egypt. As chapter four has reported extensively, the Mubarak regime, by including women from the NDP in Parliament through the quota system, corroded people's trust toward women's capacities of independently engaging in politics. These visions are shared by both men and women, showing how patriarchy and hegemonic masculine visions of power have soaked the minds of both genders alike. Egyptians, however, seem to deny the existence of a resilient patriarchy within Egyptian society, pointing at economic and social instability as the main reasons for women's problems. This has been, for instance, remarked in the case of women's harassment on March 8, an event that has been explained as the sign of a wide-ranging sense of frustration and powerlessness among many young Egyptians.

On the contrary, some other respondents have blamed families, which do not support and help women who want to be active in public work, considering it shameful for a woman to act as a leader. As someone has reported, the environment in which women still live makes them followers and not leaders. Measuring the success of a woman is not about her career or qualifications as a worker, but by getting married and becoming a mother. The respondents to the survey seem to have, on the contrary, a much more positive perspective, and a high percentage disagree with the idea that politics is a male-only field. However, almost 60 percent of male survey respondents still remained anchored to the idea that a woman cannot be president of the country, confirming that gender divisions persevere unchanged within popular mentality.

As this work has also underlined, the widespread unawareness of both men and women about the Personal Status Laws and women's rights under the law is remarkable. This confirms the tendency that, for normal Egyptians, these issues do not represent daily priorities and therefore are not further investigated. Only the widely debated *khul'* law still inflames the debate. For several women who participated in this research, the *khul'* law, as introduced under the direction of Suzanne Mubarak, gave more rights to women than those stated in the prophetic *hadith*. The current form of *khul'* takes away men's unilateral right to ask for divorce, and a diverse interpretation of the *khul'* should be implemented, according to which women can divorce themselves after previous consent from their husbands. Women, indeed, being emotional beings, should have a much more limited access to divorce than men, as some respondents have argued. On the contrary, for a few others, the Personal Status Laws remain deeply discriminatory against women, as they have been modeled according to men's views and needs. The statistics of the survey are instead slightly different. Women are overall more in favor of the *khul'*, while men are more against it.

As for reforming the custody law, the majority of respondents seem to be unified around the need of giving fathers more time with their children. However, some Egyptians believe that children might suffer from psychological problems when separated for too long from their fathers, while for others, the law is not compatible with *Shari'a,* as it gives mothers more time with their children and is discriminatory against fathers.

Overall, Egyptians are absolutely much more open now to debate than before, and this is shown by the great response that the topic of this work has received among men and women of all social classes and political affiliations. But Egyptian society unquestionably has not changed its patriarchal and masculine nature, and religion still represents the pole around which any argument in relation to women still turns around. Cultural conservatism, reinforced by religious beliefs more than political ideas, informs people's thinking and inhibits women's equality in all areas of civil life. Thus, as Botman argues, "Gender relations will remain uneven until conventional social beliefs are jettisoned and the full meaning of women's citizenship in social, economic and political life embraced" (Botman 1999, 114). The serious problems that women face will never be surmounted until gender issues will not be included in a broader society-wide discourse.

5.4 A new beginning?

In the days when this work was close to its end, some events of unprecedented relevance happened in late December 2011. During clashes between army soldiers and demonstrators asking the SCAF to step down, several women were harassed and abused by soldiers near Tahrir Square. On more than one occasion, soldiers grabbed and stripped female demonstrators, even tearing off their headscarves. In one specific case, several soldiers beat and kicked a supine woman and ripped off her *abaya* to reveal a blue bra (Kirkpatrick 2011). Therefore, in the afternoon of December 20, around 10,000 women, supported by men and university students, marched in the streets of central Cairo demanding that Egypt's ruling military step down, an unprecedented show of outrage over soldiers' attacks on female activists. The march, organized by the Mohamed El-Baradei Campaign and the April 6 Youth Movement, reached the Journalists Syndicate, where, in 2005, several female protesters were sexually assaulted by Interior Ministry thugs.

Female protesters chanted slogans against the violence of the SCAF and the marginalization of women in the political transitional period. They showed their support for Ghada Kamal Abdel Razek, the woman that was dragged out in the street by the armed forces. Among others, one of the slogans said, "Girls of Egypt are a red line," reclaiming their right to protest and express themselves (Carr 2011).

A few hours after the march took place, SCAF apologized for the violations. One public statement read, "The SCAF reaffirms its upmost respect and admiration for the women of Egypt and their right to protest and of positive participation in political life on the path of democratic change Egypt is currently witnessing and all legal measures have been taken to hold officials accountable for transgressions" (Ibid.). Twenty-nine groups and parties also called for mass demonstrations on Friday, December 23, in which women participated to condemn aggressions against women protesters as a result of the events at the Ministerial Cabinet.

Thus, for the academic purpose of this work, this protest march was noteworthy for several reasons. It represents the first genuine and spontaneous movement of women since the beginning of the revolution. This demonstration seems far away from the events of March 8 during International Women's Day, when female activists were harassed by men in Tahrir Square. The two events were undoubtedly different in scope and demands. While on March 8, feminists and women's rights activists from groups and NGOs were mainly asking for women-only-based demands a few days after Mubarak had stepped down, this protest instead was the collective reaction of ordinary Egyptian women of all ages and social classes asking for dignity, respect, and freedom. Besides, while on March 8, women's demands were seen as an unjustified act of aggression against men and an attempt to divide people's demands, this time, women marched alongside men toward a common cause: that of asking for the end of SCAF's control, and political freedom and justice. These women do not consider themelves feminists or women's rights activists, but they are simply courageous women who represent the vast majority of the Egyptian female population which does not want to be categorized under any feminist flag.

Another event that, in late December, also gathered hundreds of women and men in the streets was during the day of the court case session that took place to bring in a verdict on the "virginity tests." Samira Ibrahim, one of the many women subjected to the tests, filed a lawsuit against the military police in early March. The case sparked controversy in Egyptian society after Samira's bravery to publicly report the violations of such humiliating acts by the military, which made the case of "virginity tests" an issue of public opinion. During the court session, hundreds of people demonstrated in solidarity with Samira, holding signs that read, "Egypt's women are a red line." The people applauded and cheered upon hearing the verdict, which favored Samira and confirmed the illegality of virginity tests on any female detainee.

Women's demonstrations were not the result of any call by feminist groups or women NGOs, but the spontaneous participation of women who believe in the values of freedom and justice. On both occasions, Egyptian women did not mobilize through a feminist appeal, but a series of common political and ideological beliefs. Therefore, in the coming period, it will be fundamental for the several feminist groups and women's NGOs to strategically and politically support this nascent women's mass movement and its requests for social justice and democracy.

[72]

5.5 Need of further research

This research was limited in scope and finalized in the period between January and August 2011. Because the research study of this book was small in size and conducted exclusively in Cairo, it will be imperative to validate this research with new quantitative and qualitative studies by focusing future investigation on other areas of the country, as well by enlarging the scope of this research. With the revolution still in progress and with ongoing rounds of elections, many recent developments did not find space in this book. Thus, it would be of utmost interest to examine the future of the movement and its strategies, and to see how women's requests will be answered by the new government. With the overwhelming victory of Islamists in the parliamentary elections, the coming period will absolutely represent an interesting area of research in order to investigate how the "woman question" will be addressed by the new forces in power, and which strategies the several women's groups and coalitions will employ to address the future needs of the Egyptian women.

LIST OF REFERENCES

Blog articles

Awadalla, Ahmed. "Opportunistic Islamists and women rights in transitional Egypt." *Rebel with a cause,* 30 April 2011. Blog. Available from: http://rwac-egypt.blogspot.com/2011/04/opportunistic-islamists-and-women.html (accessed 5 October, 2011)

Badran, Margot. "Uprising in Egypt: Egyptian Revolution and the new Feminism." *The Immanent Frame: secularism, religion and the public sphere,* 3 March 2011. Blog. Available from: http://blogs.ssrc.org/tif/2011/03/03/egypts-revolution-and-the-new-feminism/ (accessed 8 May, 2011)

Bowman, Warigia. "Which Egyptian parties represent women and Copts and young people?" *Democratizing the New Egypt,* 15 November 2011. Blog. Available from: http://democratizingegypt.blogspot.com/2011/11/which-egyptian-parties-represent-women.html (accessed 22 November, 2011)

David. "Egyptian SCAF unveils new electoral system." *Democracy & Society.* 24 July 2011. Blog. Available from: http://

www.democracyandsociety.com/blog/2011/07/24/egyptian-scaf-unveils-new-electoral-system/ (accessed 10 October, 2011)

Rabbani, Hanan. "Why are women shut out of Egypt's Constitutional Committee?" *Open Society Foundation*, 25 February 2011. Blog. Available from: http://blog.soros.org/2011/02/why-are-women-shut-out-of-egypts-constitutional-committee/ (accessed 18 March, 2011)

Books & chapters of books

Abu-Lughod, Lila. 2008. *Writing Women's Worlds: Bedouin Stories*. Berkeley: University of California Press.

Afkhami, Mahnaz and Erika Friedl (eds). 1994. *In the Eye of the Storm. Women in Post-Revolutionary Iran.* London: I.B. Tauris & Co Ltd.

Ahmed, Leila. 1993. *Women and Gender in Islam: Historical Roots of a Modern Debate.* Cairo: The American University in Cairo Press.

Al-Ali, Nadje Sadig. 2000. *Secularism, Gender and the State in the Middle East: The Egyptian Women's Movement.* Cambridge, United Kingdom: Cambridge University Press.

Amin, Gamal. 2011. *Egypt in the Era of Hosni Mubarak 1981-2011.* Cairo: The American University in Cairo Press.

Amin, Qasim. 1995. *The New Woman: A Document in the Early Debate on Egyptian Feminism.* Cairo: The American University in Cairo Press.

Arabi, Oussama. 2001. *Studies in Modern Islamic Law and Jurisprudence.* The Hague: Kluwer Law International.
Badran, Margot. 1996. *Feminists, Islam and Nation: Gender and the Making of Modern Egypt.* Cairo: The American University in Cairo Press.

-------------------- 2009. *Feminism in Islam: secular and religious convergences.* Oxford: Oneworld.

Baker, Alison. 1998. *Voices of Resistance. Oral Histories of Moroccan Women.* New York: State University of New York Press.

Baron, Beth. 2005. *Egypt as a Woman: Nationalism, Gender, and Politics.* Berkeley: University of California Press.

----------------- 1994. *The Women's Awakening in Egypt: Culture, Society, and the Press.* New Haven: Yale University Press.

Bayat, Asef. 2009. *Life as politics: How Ordinary people change the Middle East.* Cairo: The American University in Cairo Press.

Botman, Selma. 1999. *Engendering Citizenship in Egypt.* New York: Columbia University Press.

Charrad, Mounira. 2001. *States and women's rights: the making of postcolonial Tunisia, Algeria, and Morocco.* University of California Press.

Dunne, Tim, Milja Kurki and Steve Smith. 2007. *International relations: discipline and diversity.* New York: Oxford University Press.

Esposito, John L. 2001. *Women in Muslim Family Law.* Syracuse, New York: Syracuse University Press.

Haddad, Yvonne Yazbeck and John L.Esposito. 1998. *Islam, Gender, & Social Change.* New York: Oxford University Press.

Hassan, Farkhonda, Sahar Nasr and Maya Morsy. 2009. *Gender Equality creates Democracy.* Cairo: National Council for Women.

Kamrava, Mehran. 2005. *The Modern Middle East: a political history since the First World War.* Berkeley: University of California Press.

Karam, Azza. 1998. *Women, Islamisms and the State: Contemporary Feminisms in Egypt.* New York: St. Martin's press.

Kassem, Maya. 2004. *Egyptian politics: the Dynamics of Authoritarian Rule.* Boulder, Colo.: Lynne Rienner Publishers.

Knauss, Peter R. 1987. *The Persistence of Patriarchy: Class, Gender, and Ideology in Twentieth Century Algeria.* New York: Praeger Publishers.

Lorber, Judith. 2010. *Gender inequality: Feminist theory and politics.* New York: Oxford University Press.

Mariscotti, Cathlyn. 2008. *Gender and Class in the Egyptian Women's Movement, 1925-1939: Changing perspectives.* New York: Syracuse University Press.

Nashat, Guity. 1983. *Women and Revolution in Iran.* Boulder, Colorado: Westview Press.

Nelson, Cynthia. 1996. *Doria Shafik, Egyptian Feminist: A Woman Apart.* Cairo: The American University in Cairo Press.

Rutherford, Bruce K. 2008. *Egypt after Mubarak: Liberalism, Islam, and Democracy in the Arab.* Princeton: Princeton University Press.

Sedghi, Hamideh. 2007. *Women and Politics in Iran: veiling, unvelining, and reveiling.* Cambridge: Cambridge University Press.

Singerman, Diane and Homa Hoodfar. 1996. *Development, change, and gender in Cairo: a view from the household.* Bloomington: Indiana University Press.

Sullivan, Earl L. 1986. *Women in Egyptian Public Life.* New York: Syracuse University Press.

Supplee, Joan. 1994. "Women and the Counter-Revolution in

Chile" in Tetreault, Mary Ann (ed.) 1994. *Women and the Revolution in Africa, Asia, and the New World*. Columbia, S.C.: University of South Carolina Press.

Tarrow, Sidney. 1994. *Power in Movement-Social Movements, Collective Action and Politics*. Cambridge: Cambridge University Press in Jad, Islah. 2004. The NGO-isation of Arab Women's Movements. Institute of Development Studies Bulletin 35, Issue 4 (October).

Tetreault, Mary Ann (ed.) 1994. *Women and the Revolution in Africa, Asia, and the New World*. Columbia, S.C.: University of South Carolina Press.

Tucker, Judith E. 2008. *Women, Family, and Gender in Islamic Law*. New York: Cambridge University Press.

Warrick, Catherine. 2009. *Law in the Service of Legitimacy. Gender and Politics in Jordan*. Farnham, England: Ashgate Pub.

Waylen, Georgina. 2007. *Engendering transitions*. New York: Oxford University Press.

Conference proceedings

El-Nakash, Farida. 2011. "The Egyptian revolution: the position of women related to secularism and the role of syndicates." Associacio' Catalunya-Liban. http://www.contemporania.org/monarab/EL-NAKASH,%20The%20Egyptian%20Revolution.pdf

Fay, Mary Ann. 2003. International Feminism and the Women's Movement in Egypt, 1904-1923. A Reappraisal of Categories and Legacies. Presented at the Conference on Institutions, Ideologies and Agencies Changing Family Life in the Arab Middle East, University of North Carolina at Chapel Hill, April, North Carolina.

Hodkinson, Phil and H. Hodkinson. 2001. The Strengths and Limitations of Empirical study Research. Paper presented to the learning and skills development agency conference "Making an impact on policy and practice" University of Leeds, England.

Journal articles

Abdel Latif, Omayma. 2008. In the Shadow of the Brothers: The Egyptian of the Muslim Brotherhood. *Carnegie endowment for the Middle East,* no.13 (October): 1-23.

Al-Ali, Nadje Sadig. 2002. The Women's Movement in Egypt, with Selected References to Turkey. *UNRISD, Civil Society and Social Movements Programme,* no.5 (April): 1-37.

Amrane-Minne, Danièle Djamila and Farida Abu-Haidar. 1999. Women and Politics in Algeria from the war of Independence to our day. *Research in African Literatures* 30, no. 3, Dissident Algeria (autumn): 62-77.

Bernard-Maugiron. 2008. Breaking-off the Family: Divorce in Egyptian Law and Practice. *Hawwa* no.6: 52-74.

Coleman, Isobel. 2011. On the Front Lines of Change: Women in the Arab Uprisings. Policy brief, *Project on Middle East Democracy* (July): 1-6.

Cooke, Miriam. 1989. Deconstructing war discourse: Women's Participation in the Algerian Revolution. *Duke University Working Paper,* no.184 (June): 1-26.

El-Mahdi, Rabab. 2010. Does Political Islam impede Gender-Based Mobilization? The Case of Egypt. *Totalitarian Movements and Political Religions* 11, no. 3-4: 379-396.

Geschwender, James A. 1968. Explorations in the Theory of Social Movements and Revolutions. *Social Forces* 47, no. 2 (December): 127-135.

Ghosh, Huma Ahmed. 2008. Dilemma of Islamic and Secular Feminists and Feminisms. *Journal of International Women's Studies* 9, no.3 (May): 99-116.

Graham-Brown, Sarah. 1981. Feminism in Egypt: A Conversation with Nawal Sadawi. MERIP Reports, no.95 (Mar-Apr): 24-27.

Halper, Louise. 2005. Law and Women's Agency in Post- Revolutionary Iran. *Harvard Journal of Law & Gender* 28, no. 85 (winter): 86-142.

Hassim, Shireen. 2002. "A Conspiracy of Women": the Women's Movement in South Africa's Transition to Democracy. *Social Research* 69, no. 3, the Status of Women in the Developing World (fall): 693-732.

Hatem, Mervat. 1986. The Enduring Alliance of Nationalism and Patriarchy in Muslim Personal Status Laws: The Case of Modern Egypt. *Feminist Issues* 6, no.1: 19-43.

Hussein, Aziza. 1953. The Role of Women in Social Reform in Egypt. *Middle East Journal* 7, no.4 (autumn): 440-450.

Jad, Islah. 2004. The NGO-isation of Arab Women's Movements. Institute of Development Studies Bulletin 35, Issue 4 (October).

Mashhour, Amira. 2005. Islamic Law and Gender Equality–Could there be a Common Ground? A study of Divorce and Polygamy in Sharia Law and Contemporary Legislation in Tunisia and Egypt. *Human Rights Quarterly* 7, no. 27, John Hopkins University Press (May): 562-596.

Mohammadi, Majid. 2007. Iranian Women and the Civil Rights Movement in Iran: Feminism Interacted. *Journal of International Women's Studies* 9, no. 1 (November): 1-21.

Naveh, Immanuel. 2001. The Tort of Injury and Dissolution of

Marriage at the Wife's Initiative in Egyptian *Maḥkamat Al-Naqḍ* Rulings. *Islamic Law and Society* 9, no.1: 16-41.

Paonessa, Costantino. 2008. Il diritto di famiglia in Egitto: lo "Stato" nel ruolo di interprete della Legge Islamica. *Cultura. International Journal of Philosophy of Culture and Axiology* 10 (October): 14-28.

Peterson, V. Spike. 1998. Feminisms and International Relations. *Gender & History* 10, no.3 (November): 581–589.

Sadiqi, Fatima and Moha Ennaji. 2006. The Feminization of Public Space: Women's Activism, the Family Law, and Social Change in Morocco. *Journal of Middle East Women's Studies* 2, no. 2, Special Issue: Women's Activism and the Public Sphere (spring): 86-114.

Seidman, Gay W. 1999. Gendered Citizenship: South Africa's Democratic Transition and the Construction of a Gendered State. *Gender and Society* 13, no. 3 (June): 287-307.

Social Research Association. 2003. Ethical guidelines. (December): 1-64.

Soufi, Hana. 2009. Parliamentary democracy and the representation of women in Arab countries. *Contemporary Arab Affairs* 2, no. 2 (April-June): 252-271.

Tadros, Mariz. 2011. The Muslim Brotherhood's Gender Agenda: Reformed or Reframed? *IDS Bulletin* 42, no. 1 (January): 88-98.

Tanter, Raymond and Manus Midlarsky. 1967. A Theory of Revolution. *The Journal of Conflict Resolution* 11, no.3 (September): 264-280.

Tellis, Winston. 1997. Application of an Empirical study Methodology. *The Qualitative Report* 3, no.3 (September). http://www.nova.edu/ssss/QR/QR3-3/tellis2.html

Turshen, Meredeth. 2002. Algerian Women in the Liberation Struggle and the Civil War: From Active Participants to Passive Victims? *Social Research* 69, no.3 (fall): 890-911.

Waylen, Georgina. 2000. Gender and Democratic Politics: A Comparative Analysis of Consolidation in Argentina and Chile. *Journal of Latin American Studies* 32, no. 3 (October): 765-793.

----------------------2010. Gendering politics and policy in transitions to democracy: Chile and South Africa. *Policy & Politics* 38, no. 3 (February): 337–52.

----------------------1994. Women and Democratization: Conceptualizing gender relations in Transition Politics. *World Politics* 46, no. 3 (April): 327-354.

Newspaper and magazine articles

Abdel Aziz, Essam. Raṣd: al-eʿlāmiyya Būthayna Kāmel toʿlen tarashoḥaha li-re'āset al-jomhūryya (Media: Bothaina Kamel announces her candidacy for the elections). *Al Shorouk*, 3 April 2011. Newspaper-online. Available from: http://www.shorouknews.com/contentdata.aspx?id=422618 (accessed June 7, 2011)

Abdel Hafiz, Heba. 'ʿlamā' al-sharīʿa wa al-qānūn: qwānīn Sūzān dammarit al-'osra al-maṣryya (Sharia scholars and law: the laws of Suzanne destroyed the Egyptian family). *Ikwan online*, 28 April 2011. Newspaper-online. Available from: http://www.ikhwanonline.com/new/Article.aspx?ArtID=83338&SecID=323 (accessed May 15, 2011)

Abdel Hamid Hafez, Fathy. Qūtat al-mar'a baʿd 25 yanāyer bayna al-ebqā' wa al-ilghā' (The future of the quota after the revolution of the 25th of January). *Sut el-Hurriya* (Voice of Freedom), 13 March 2011. Newspaper-online. Available from: http://

www.baghdadtimes.net/Arabic/?sid=70697 (accessed May 5, 2011)

Abdel Rahman, Walid. Al-āzhar yastajīb liḍoghūṭ al-tayyār al-salafī wa yoqarrer tashkīl lajna limorājaʿet qwānīn al-aḥwāl al-shakhsiyya (Azhar responds to the pressure of the Salafis and de-cide to form a committee to review the Personal Status Laws). *Asharq Al Awsat*, 17 May 2011. Newspaper-online. Available from: http://www.aawsat.com/details.asp?section=17&issueno=11858&article=622028 (accessed June 20, 2011)

Abdoun, Safaa. Army Council approves Sexual Harassment Law. *The Daily News Egypt*, April 1 2011. Newspaper-online. Avail-able from: http://www.thedailynewsegypt.com/army-council-approves-sexual-harassment-law.html (accessed June 4, 2011)

Abuelgar, Mona. Makāsib al-mara' fī khatar (Women's gains at risk). *Al-Ahram Daily*, 18 may 2011. Newspaper-online. Available from: http://digital.ahram.org.eg/Community.aspx?Serial=509229 (accessed July 7, 2011)

Abu Sakin, Mona. Hezb si al-Sayed yaʿūd bi-'amina ila al-manzel (The party si el Said invites to the safety of the home). *El Wafd*, 17 April 2011. Newspaper-online. Available from: http://wafdnews.com/index.php?option=com_content&view=article&id=35048:%D8%AD%D8%B2%D8%A8%E2%80%AE-%E2%80%AC%D8%B3%D9%8A-%D8%A7%D9%84%D8%B3%D9%8A%D8%AF%E2%80%AE-%E2%80%AC%D9%8A%D8%B9%D9%88%D8%AF-%D8%A8%D9%80-%D8%A3%D9%85%D9%8A%D9%86%D8%A9%E2%80%AE-%E2%80%AC%D8%A5%D9%84%D9%8A-%D8%A7%D9%84%D9%85%D9%86%D8%B2%D9%84&catid=131:%D8%A7%D9%84%D8%B5%D9%81%D8%AD%D9%87%20%D8%A7%D9%84%D8%A7%D8%AE%D9%8A%D8%B1%D9%87&Itemid=370#axzz1N0av6WJi (accessed

June 18, 2011)

Afify, Heba. Naguib Sawiris launches liberal "Free Egyptian Party." *Al Masry Al Youm*, English Edition, 4 April 2011. Newspaper-online. Available from: http://www.almasryalyoum.com/en/node/386398 (accessed October 9, 2011)

Afify, Heba. "Virginity text victims lodges official complaint with military." *Al Masry Al Youm*, 30 June 2011. Newspaper-online. Available from: http://www.almasryalyoum.com/en/node/473319 (accessed July 4, 2011)

Ahmed, Heba. Moẓāhara le-ta'dīl qānūn al-ro'ya (Demonstration to amend the custody law). *Al Wafd*, 23 March 2011. Newspaper-online. Available from: http://www.alwafd.org/-الصفحة الاخيرة/79-الصفحه20%الاخيره/26420-مظاهرة-لتعديل-قانون-الرؤية (accessed April 24, 2011)

Ahram online. Salafists to protest court ruling banning *niqab* during exams. 24 April 2011. Newspaper-online. Available from: http://english.ahram.org.eg/NewsContent/1/64/10708/Egypt/Politics-/Salafists-to-protest-court-ruling-banning-niqab-du.aspx (accessed October 10, 2011)

--------------- Tunisia to give women candidates parity with men in polls. 12 April, 2011. Newspaper-online. Available from: http://english.ahram.org.eg/NewsContent/2/8/9851/World/Region/Tunisia-to-give-women-candidates-parity-with-men-i.aspx (accessed June 16, 2011)

Al Bahery, Ahmed. Me'āt al-montaqebāt wa al-salafeyīn yataẓaharūn 'amām "mashyakhet al-azhar" ḍeḍ fatwā "Gom'a (Hundreds of veiled women and Salafis protest against the Azhar *fatwa* against *niqab*). *Al Masry Al Youm*, 6 May 2011. Newspaper-online. Available from: http://www.almasryalyoum.com/article2.aspx?ArticleID=295887&IssueID=2127 (accessed July 13, 2011)

Al Gali, Magdi. Sharaf yaṭlob al-mashūra fī: tafʿīl dūr al-mara' (Sharaf consults the women movement on the role of women). Al *Youm El-Sabe3*, 28 June 2011. Newspaper-online. Available from: http://www.youm7.com/News.asp? NewsID=444439&SecID=65 (accessed July 28, 2011)

Ali, Eman. Al-dākhīlyya towafeq ʿala manḥ al-jensyya le-abnā' al-motazawwejāt min falasṭīnyīn (Interior approved the granting of citizenship to the children of women married to Palestinians).Al *Youm El-Sabe3*, 3 May 2011. Newspaper-online. Available from: http://www.youm7.com/News.asp? NewsID=404069 (accessed October 2, 2011)

Ali, Loa'y. Mojammʿ al-boḥoth al-eslāmyya yonāqesh qawānīn al-ṭefl wa al-'osra (Islamic research Academy discusses the laws of the child and family) *Al Youm El-Sabe3*, 26 April 2011. News-paper-online. Available from: http://save-thefamily.blogspot.com/2011/04/blog-post_26.html (accessed October 6, 2011)

Al-markaz al-maṣrī li-ḥoqūq al-mara': li-taḥqīq tamṯīl ʿadel li-al-nesā' fī al- majāles al-montakhaba (Egyptian Center for Women's Rights: to achieve a fair representation of women in elected bodies). *Islam Times*, 7 April 2011. News-paper-online. Available from: http://www.islamtimes.org/vdcdxj09.yt0ss6242y.html (accessed September 21, 2011)

Al-Sharmani, Mulki. Egypt's family courts: route to empower-ment? *Open Democracy*, 2007. http://www.opendemocracy.net/article/egypt_and_family_law (accessed July 5, 2010)

Al-Tagammoʿ yarfoḍ taʿdīlāt qanūn al-barlamān wa yor-aḥḥeb bi elghā' qotat al-mara' (Tagammu rejects the People's Assemble Law and the quota for women). *Misr El Ge-dida*, 31 May, 2011. Newspaper-online. Available from: http://www.misrelgdida.com/Parties/62395.html (accessed June 30,

2011)

Amar, Paul. Egypt after Mubarak. *The Nation*, May 4 2011. Newspaper-online. Available from: http://www.thenation.com/article/160439/egypt-after-mubarak?page=0%2C0 (accessed June16, 2011)

Awad, Marwa and Hugo Dixon. Special report: Inside the Egyptian Revolution. *Reuters,* U.S. edition, April 13 2011. Newspaper-online. Available from: http://www.reuters.com/article/2011/04/13/us-egypt-revolution-idUSTRE73C18E20110413 (accessed June16, 2011)

Bryjak, George J. The making of a revolution. *Adirondach Daily Enterprise,* 23 February 2011. Newspaper-online. Available from: http://www.adirondackdailyenterprise.com/page/content.detail/id/523131.html67yyyyyyyyyyyy% (accessed March 19, 2011)

Būthayna Kāmel morashaḥet al-Re'asa toṭleq qanā fḍā'yya jadīda qarīban (Bothaina Kamel Presidential Candidate launches a new satellite channel). *El Shorouk*, 30 April 2011. Newspaper-online. Available from: http://www.shorouknews.com/ContentData.aspx?id=444052 (accessed June 2, 2011)

Carr, Sarah. Women march against SCAF brutality, hope for a nascent movement. *Egypt Independent*, 20 December 2011. Newspaper-online. Available from: http://www.almasryalyoum.com/en/node/559926 (accessed December 21, 2011)

CBS News' Lara Logan Assaulted During Egypt Protests. *60 Minutes*, 15 February 2011. Newspaper-online. Available from:http://www.cbsnews.com/stories/2011/02/15/60minutes/main20032070.shtml (accessed March 2, 2011)

Clark, Michael. Rising Feminism bewilders Egypt. *ProQuest Historical Newspapers, The New York Times* (1851 - 2007), 5 March 1951.

Dawood, Alia. Backlash against 'Suzanne Mubarak laws' was inevitable. *Egypt Independent*, 8 November 2011. Newspaper-online. Available from: http://www.almasryalyoum.com/en/node/512796 (accessed November 25, 2011)

Egypt News Hub. Salafis protest for release of alleged convert to Islam. *Egypt News Hub*, 19 April 2011. Newspaper-online. Available from: http://www.egyptnewshub.com/index.php/egypt-news/3471-salafis-protest-for-release-of-alleged-convert-to-islam.html (accessed June 7, 2011)

Elhabbal, Ayat. ʿAmr Mūsa: ḥoqūq al-mara' mojarrad show li-hezb al-sayyda al-ʿūla (Amr Moussa: women rights are that benefited the First Lady) *Al Wafd*, 23 August 2011. Newspaper-online. Available from: http://www.alwafd.org/%D8%A3%D8%B3%D8%B1%D8%A9/84-%D9%87%D9%88%20%D9%88%20%D9%87%D9%89/86343-%D8%B9%D9%85%D8%B1%D9%88-%D9%85%D9%88%D8%B3%D9%89-%D8%AD%D9%82%D9%88%D9%82-%D8%A7%D9%84%D9%85%D8%B1%D8%A3%D8%A9-%D9%85%D8%AC%D8%B1%D8%AF-%D9%88-%D9%84%D8%AD%D8%B3%D8%A7%D8%A8-%D8%A7%D9%84%D8%B3%D9%8A%D8%AF%D8%A9-%D8%A7%D9%84%D8%A3%D9%88%D9%84%D9%89 (accessed October 4, 2011)

El-Wakil, Mai. Fallen faces of the uprising: Sally Zahran. *Al Masry Al Youm* (English edition), 7 February 2011. Newspaper-online. Available from: http://www.almasryalyoum.com/en/node/311971 (accessed 5 May, 2011)

Elyan, Tamim. Muslim Sisterhood holds first conference in 60 years. *The Daily News Egypt*, 3 July 2011. Newspaper-online. Available from: http://thedailynewsegypt.com/egypt/muslim-sisterhood-holds-first-conference-in-60-years.html (accessed July 16, 2011)

Fadel, Leila. Asmaa Mahfouz, Egyptian youth activist, is charged by military prosecutor. *The Washington World Post,* 15 August 2011. Newspaper-online. Available from: http://www.washingtonpost.com/world/middle-east/asmaa-mahfouz-egyptian-youth-activist-is-charged-by-military-prosecutor/2011/08/14/gIQAuqihFJ_story.html (accessed August 18, 2011)

Fahmy, Heba and Tamim Elyan. Freedom and Justice Party submits documents, includes over 900 women, 93 Copts. *The Daily News Egypt*, 18 may 2011. Newspaper-online. Available from: http://www.thedailynewsegypt.com/egypt/freedom-and-justice-party-submits-documents-includes-over-900-women-93-copts.html (accessed June 8, 2011)

Fahmy, Maysa. Al-moftī ya'ed be-fatwa ḥawla qanūn al-ro'ya (The Mufti calls for a Fatwa for the law on custody). *El Shorouk,* 18 April 2011. Newspaper-online. Available from: http://www.shorouknews.com/ContentData.aspx?id=434884 (accessed June 12, 2011)

Fahmy, Maysa. (b) Ra'īs maḥkamet al-'osra yattahem Sūzān Mubārak be-'efsād al-'osra al-maṣreyya (The President of the Family Court accused Suzanne Mubarak of having corrupted the Egyptian family). *El Shorouk,* 28 April 2011. Newspaper-online. Available from: http://www.shorouknews.com/ContentData.aspx?id=442580 (accessed June 2, 2011)

Haitham Al-Sharkawi and Emad Khalil. Orthodox Church denies attacking Coptic protesters with dogs. *Al Masry Al Youm*, 21 July 2011. Newspaper-online. Available from: http://www.almasryalyoum.com/en/node/479173 (accessed October 10, 2011)

Hosea, Leana. A Woman's place in the New Egypt. *BBC News Middle East*, 23 March 2011. Newspaper-online. Available from: http://www.bbc.co.uk/news/world-middle-east-12819919 (accessed April 18, 2011)

Kandiyoti, Deniz. Promise and peril: women and the 'Arab spring. *Open Democracy*, http://www.opendemocracy.net/5050/deniz-kandiyoti/promise-and-peril-women-and-%E2%80%98arab-spring%E2%80%99 (accessed September 13, 2011)

Khalil, Fatima. Huda Badrān: ḥokomat sharaf tastab'ed al-mara' (Huda Badran: The government of women excluded women). *Al Youm El Sabe3*, 4 June 2011. Newspaper-online. Available from: http://www.youm7.com/News.asp?NewsID=428115&SecID=97&IssueID=168 (accessed June 8, 2011)

Kings and Cabbages. Egypt's revolution: causes and triggers. *Word Press*, 28 January 2011. Newspaper-online. Available from: http://kingsandcabbages.wordpress.com/2011/01/28/egypts-revolution-causes-and-triggers/ (accessed March 3, 2011)

Kirkpatrick, David D. Mass March by Cairo Women in Protest Over Abuse by Soldiers. *The New York Times*, 20 December 2011. Newspaper-online. Available from: http://www.nytimes.com/2011/12/21/world/middleeast/violence-enters-5th-day-as-egyptian-general-blames-protesters.html?_r=2&pagewanted=all (accessed December 23, 2011)

Latif, Ahmed. Al-majles al-waṭanī yo'len waṭiqat al-dostūr wa yoṭāleb be-dawla madaneyya (The National council declares the Constitution and calls for a civil state). *Masrawy*, 3 July 2011. Newspaper-online. Available from: http://www.masrawy.com/news/egypt/politics/2011/july/3/

new_country.aspx?ref=moreclip (accessed October 2, 2011)

Leila, Reem. Controversy over 'Suzanne's laws'. *Al-Ahram Weekly*, 5-11 May 2011. Newspaper-online. Available from: http://weekly.ahram.org.eg/2011/1046/eg14.htm (accessed October 6, 2011)

Magdi, Basma. Äawret rejāl miṣr "tad'ū li-waqfa selmyya amam wezāret al-'adel (Men of Egyptian revolution calls for a peaceful protest in front of the Ministry of Justice). *Al Youm Al Sabe3*, 12 June 2011. Newspaper-online. Available from: http://www.youm7.com/News.asp?NewsID=433659&SecID=65&IssueID=0 (accessed July 1, 2011)

Magdi, Osama. Masīra li-al-salafyyīn bi-al-qāhera wa 'okhra be-al-'eskandaryya li-al-moṭālaba bi-al-'efrāj 'an Kamelya (March of the Salafists in Cairo and Alexandria to demand the release of "Camelia). *Al Masry Al Youm*, 30 March, 2011. Newspaper-online. Available from: http://www.almasry-alyoum.com/article2.aspx?ArticleID=295281&IssueID=2121 (accessed May 15, 2011)

Mansour, Kamel. Majles al-wozarā' yo'len al-youm 'eqalet al-qeyādāt al-ḥokomyya al- montamyya li-al -waṭanī wa al-moṭa-warreṭīn fī qaḍaya fasād (Council of Ministers today announces dismissal of government leaders involved in corrupted cases). *Al Masry Al Youm*, 27 July 2011. Newspaper-online. Available from: http://www.almasryalyoum.com/article2.aspx?ArticleID=305274&IssueID=2209 (accessed October 11, 2011)

Mekay, Emad. Arab women lead the charge for political change. *The Electronic Intifada*, 13 of February 2011. Newspaper-online. Available from: http://electronicintifada.net/content/arab-women-lead-charge-political-change/9807 (accessed March 12, 2011)

Michael, Maggie. Constitutional Amendments approved in

Egypt referendum. *The star*, 20 March 2011. Newspaper-online. Available from: http://www.thestar.com/news/world/article/956926--constitutional-amendments-approved-in-egypt-referendum (accessed May 7, 2011)

Minister: No female governors to be appointed in planned reshuffle. *Al Masry Al Youm*, 30 July 2011. Newspaper-online. Available from: http://www.almasryalyoum.com/en/node/481744 (accessed August 5, 2011)

Miṣr: ḍamān damj ḥoqūq al-mara' fī Miṣr ma baʿd al-ṯawra (Ensure the integration of women's rights in Egypt after the revolution.) *Equality now*, 10 July 2011. Newspaper-online. Available from: http://equalitynow.org/ar/take_action/action381 (accessed October 2, 2011)

Nabil, Aya. Al-jamʿyyāt al-ahlyya toʿlen ta'sīs taḥalof li-al-taʿlīm al-madaney wa moshāraket al-mar'a (NGOs announce the establishment of the Coalition for Civic Education and Women's Participation). *Al Youm El Sabe3*, 22 February 2011. Newspaper-online. Available from: http://www.youm7.com/News.asp?NewsID=356632 (accessed March 26, 2011)

Naib, Fatma. A long battle ahead for Egyptian Women. *Middle East*, March 9 2011. Newspaper-online. Available from: http://blogs.aljazeera.net/middle-east/2011/03/09/long-battle-ahead-egyptian-women (accessed April 23, 2011)

Nasser, Wafae. Moẓāhara amām Masbīrū li-ʿelghā' qānūn ro'yat al-ṭefl (Dispersion of the child because of the custody law). *Egypt News, Akbar Masr*, 11 April 2011. Newspaper-online. Available from: http://www.egynews.net/wps/portal/news?params=121032 (accessed July 7, 2011)

Nazra. Egypt: NGOs condemn personal status law decree project by president of Family Appeal Court. *Women living under Muslim Laws*, 25 July 2011.Newspaper-online. Available from: http://www.wluml.org/node/7456 (accessed August 12, 2011)

Nazra. Statement from the Coalition of Women's NGO's in Egypt. *Open Democracy*, 20 February 2011. http://www.opendemocracy.net/statement-from-coalition-of-womens-ngos-in-egypt (accessed March 18, 2011)

Noor, Naseema. Tunisia: The revolution that started it all. *International Affairs Review,* 31 January 2011. Newspaper-online. Available from: http://www.iar-gwu.org/node/257 (accessed March 12, 2011)

Othman, Dalia. Military source: Law removes quota for women in Parliament, denies vote for expats. *RSS Egypt*, 12 May 2011. Newspaper-online. Available from: http://rssmasr.com/en/military-source-law-removes-quota-for-women-in-parliament-denies-vote-for-expats/ (accessed July 7, 2011)

Owen, Margaret. Egypt, from equality of purpose to equality on the ground. *Inclusive democracy*, 1 March 2011. Newspaper-online. Available from: http://www.opendemocracy.net/5050/margaret-owen/egypt-from-equality-of-purpose-to-equality-on-ground (accessed April 12, 2011)

Parks, Cara. Arab revolutions: from Tunisia to Egypt, is this the beginning of a Trend? *Huff post world* 4 March 2011. Newspaper-online. Available from: http://www.huffingtonpost.com/2011/02/01/egypt-tunisia-arab-revolution_n_816695.html (accessed April 25, 2011)

Power, Carla. Silent no more: the Women of the Arab Revolutions. *Time World*, 24 of March 2011. Newspaper-online. Available from: http://www.time.com/time/world/article/0,8599,2059435-2,00.html (accessed May 8, 2011)

Raghavan, Sudarsan. A lost generation of young people of Tunisia discuss grievances that led to their revolution. *The Washington Post World*, 20 January, 2011. Newspaper-online. Available from: http://www.washingtonpost.com/world/a-lost-generation-of-young-people-of-tunisia-discuss-grievances-that-led-to-their-revolution/2011/01/20/ABfCqOR_story.html (accessed March 25, 2011)

Ramadan, Ahmed. 'Elghā' qotat al-mara' wa taṭbīk al-qā'ema al-nesbyya (Abolition of the quota for women and introduction of the voting list). *Ikwan online*, 11 May 2011. Newspaper-online. Available from: http://www.ikhwanonline.com/new/Article.aspx?SecID=230&ArtID=84121 (accessed June 1, 2011)

Rashwan, Hoda. Tajahol taʿyīn al- mara' f ī ḥarket al-moḥafeẓīn yofajjer al-ghaḍab
Al-nesāʿī ḍeḍ "Sharaf" (The lack of the appointment of women blows feminist anger against Sharaf) *Al Masry Al Youm*, 15 April 2011. Newspaper-online. Available from: http://www.almasryalyoum.com/node/402029 (accessed May 12, 2011)

Repubblica. Migliaia in Piazza per l'Unita' Nazionale: Arrestata Suzanne, la moglie di Mubarak. 13 may 2011. Newspaper-online. Available from: http://www.repubblica.it/esteri/2011/05/13/news/migliaia_in_piazza_tahrir-16175350/?ref=HREC1-5 (accessed June 5, 2011)

Reuters. Fact box: Egyptians want more Islam in politics: poll. *Reuters*, 2 February 2011. Newspaper-online. Available from: http://www.reuters.com/article/2011/02/02/us-egypt-islam-poll-idUSTRE7116ND20110202 (accessed October 7, 2011)

Rice, Xan. Egyptians protest over 'virginity tests' on Tahrir Square women. *The Guardian*, 31 May 2011. Newspaper-online. Available from: http://www.guardian.co.uk/world/2011/may/31/egypt-online-protest-virginity-tests (accessed July 8, 2011)

Salah, Soha. Al-jamal al-ṯawrī yoshakkel awwal ḥezb nesāʾī (The first party for women). *Al Wafd*, 12 June 2011. Newspaper-online. Available from: http://www.alwafd.org/index.php?option=com_content&view=article&id=56618:%E2%80%AE%D8%A7%D9%84%D8%AC%D9%85%D8%A7%D9%84-%D8%A7%D9%84%D8%AB%D9%88%D8%B1%D9%89-%D9%8A%D8%B4%D9%83%D9%84-%E2%80%AC%D8%A3%D9%88%D9%84-%D8%AD%D8%B2%D8%A8-%D9%86%D8%B3%D8%A7%D8%A6%D9%8A&catid=131:%D8%A7%D9%84%D8%B5%D9%81%D8%AD%D9%87%20%D8%A7%D9%84%D8%A7%D8%AE%D9%8A%D8%B1%D9%87&Itemid=370#axzz1P9dgMG6o (accessed July 8, 2011)

Samir, Sarah. E'telāf sayyedāt al-ṯawra bi-al-Eskandaryya yonaẓẓem ḥamlet eʿrafī ḥaqqeq (The coalition of revolutionary women organizes in Alexandria the campaigns "know your rights"). *Elaosboa* online, 23 June 2011. Newspaper-online. Available from: http://www.elaosboa.com/artsys00/ArticleDetails.aspx?Aid=3805 (accessed July 14, 2011)

Shaalan, Marwa. Women for more active role after Egypt's revolt. *The Egyptian Gazette Online*, 23 October 2011. Newspaper-online. Available from: http://213.158.162.45/~egyptian/index.php?action=news&id=21817&title=Women%20for%20more%20active%20role%20after%20Egypt's%20revolt (accessed December 2, 2011)

Sholkamy, Hania. Women's empowerment in the Egyptian

Revolution. *Ahram Online*, 13 February 2011. Newspaper-online. Available from: http://english.ahram.org.eg/NewsContentP/4/5517/Opinion/Women%E2%80%99s-empowerment-in-the-Egyptian-revolution.aspx (accessed July 2, 2011)

Shukrallah, Salma. Tens demonstrate for rights of Christians to civil marriage and divorce. *Ahram online*, 7 July 2011. Newspaper-online. Available from: http://english.ahram.org.eg/NewsContent/1/64/15820/Egypt/Politics-/Tens-demonstrate-for-rights-of-Christians-to-civil.aspx (accessed July 22, 2011)

Smith, Catharine. Egypt's facebook revolution: Wael Ghonim thanks the Social Network. *The Huffington Post*, 13 April 2011. Newspaper-online. Available from: http://www.huffingtonpost.com/2011/02/11/egypt-facebook-revolution-wael-ghonim_n_822078.html (accessed October 1, 2011)

Spencer, Richard. Egypt: Islamist Judge to head new constitution committee. *The Telegraph*, 15 February 2011. Newspaper-online. Available from: http://www.telegraph.co.uk/news/worldnews/africaandindianocean/egypt/8326469/Egypt-Islamist-judge-to-head-new-constitution-committee.html (accessed April 7, 2011)

Taḥālof al-monaẓẓamāṭ al-nisā'yya f ī miṣr yoṭāleb be-al-mosāwā bayna al-ragol wa al-mara' fī al-dostūr (Coalition of women's organizations in Egypt, demanding equality between men and women in the Constitution). *Radio Sawa*, 17 August 2011. Newspaper-online. Available from: http://www.radiosawa.com/article_pop.aspx?id=8063682 (accessed September 2, 2011)

Tarek, Sherif. Al-Jamaa Al-Islamiya unveils political party, voicing reservations about women's rights and secularism. *Ahram online*, 20 June 2011. Newspaper-online. Available from: http://english.ahram.org.eg/NewsContent/1/64/14695/Egypt/Politics-/AlJamaa-AlIslamiya-unveils-political-party,-voicin.aspx (accessed July 10, 2011)

Zaharan, Sahar. Dirāsat enshā' jehaz mostaqel li-shoa'ūn al-mara' wa al-ṭefl (Establishing an Independent body for Women's Affairs and Child). *Al Ahram*, 11 April 2011. Newspaper-online. Available   from: http://www.ahram.org.eg/499/2011/04/10/27/72006/219.aspx (accessed May 30, 2011)

Zaher, Abeer. Feminists form Egyptian Women Political Party. *Al Youm El-Sabae3* English Edition, 8 September 2011. Newspaper-online. Available from: http://translate.google.com.eg/translate?hl=ar&sl=en&tl=ar&u=http%3A%2F%2Fenglish.youm7.com%2FNews.asp%3FNewsID%3D344671%26SecID%3D22%26IssueID%3D0&anno=2 (accessed September 15, 2011)

Wild, Rosa. Egypt's Quiet Gender Revolution. *Think Africa Press*, 24 August 2011. Newspaper-online. Available from: http://thinkafricapress.com/egypt/egypt-quiet-gender-revolution (accessed September 13, 2011)

Wolf, Naomi. The Middle East's feminist Revolution. *Project Syndicate,* 2 March 2011. Newspaper-online. Available from: http://www.project-syndicate.org/commentary/wolf33/English (accessed March 13, 2011)

Woman at heart of sectarian clash detained. *Al Masry Al Youm*, 13 May 2011. Newspaper-online. Available from: http://www.almasryalyoum.com/en/node/435105 (accessed July 8, 2011)

Presentations

Alvarez, Sonia. June 2011. Presentation at UN Women conference: "Pathways for Women in Democratic Transitions: International Experiences and Lessons Learned."

Tadros, Mariz. June 2011. Presentation at UN Women conference: "Pathways for Women in Democratic Transitions: International Experiences and Lessons Learned."

Press releases

The Egyptian Coalition for Civic Education and Women's Participation. The cancellation of Women's Quota without alternative legal methods that guarantee women's political participation is pushing women back to the zero point. http://www.awid.org/News-Analisis/Women-s-Rights-in-the-News2/The-Egyptian-Coalition-for-Civil-Education-and-Women-s-Participation (accessed August 10, 2011)

ECWR. "Not in my name". Revolution's women strongly participate in a march against "sectarian strife" and condemn being used in it due to their religion. 10 May 2011. http://www.ecwronline.org/english/press%20reless/2011/Press%20Release-%20Not%20in%20my%20name-Revolution's%20women%20participated%20in%20a%20march%20against%20sectarian%20strife.pdf (accessed June 8, 2011)

ECWR. 80 women, human rights, and development associations in the first consultation session on Women's Commission. 23 June 2011. http://www.kvinfo.dk/file.php?file=7974 (accessed August 15, 2011)

ECWR. The Egyptian Center for Women's Rights condemns the exclusion of women from being appointed as new governors. 17 April 2011. http://www.ecwronline.org/english/press%20reless/2011/press%20release-%20women%20have%20been%20excluded%20from%20governors%20positions.pdf (accessed May 20, 2011)

Reports

Abu Dhabi Gallup Center. 2011. Egypt: the arithmetic of revolution. An empirical analyses of social and economic conditions in the months before the January 25 uprising. http://www.abudhabigallupcenter.com/147470/egypt-arithmetic-revolution.aspx

Amnesty International. 2001. Egypt rises: killings, detentions and torture in the 25 January revolution.

ECWR. Women in the news. From 22nd to 28th of July 2011. www.ecwronline.org

ECWR. Women in the news. From 8th to 14th of July 2011. www.ecwronline.org

Shrader Elizabeth and Monserrat Sagot. 2000. Domestic Violence: Women's Way Out. *Occasional Publication,* no.2, Washington D.C: PAHO.

United Nations Development Programme (UNDP). 2009. Arab Human Development Report 2009, Challenges to Human Security in the Arab Countries.

Research papers and publications

Abu-Odeh, Lama. 2010. Modernizing Muslim Family Law: the case of Egypt. Georgetown University Law Center.

Bernard-Maugiron, Nathalie. 2010. Promotion of Women's rights in Egypt. Personal Status Law in Egypt. GTZ, German Technical Cooperation. Institute of Research for Development.

Elsadda, Hoda and Emad Abu-Ghazi. 2003. Significant Moments in the History of Egyptian Women. National Council for Women, Vol. 1.

Family health International. Qualitative Research Methods: A Data Collector's Field Guide. Module 2, Participant Observation. http://www.fhi.org/NR/rdonlyres/ezacxnbfb52irvkh-kxxvf2z7vt5aglkcxlwxb3zobgbab3renayoc373plnmdyh-ga6buu5gvkcpmgl/frontmatter1.pdf

Guenena, Nemat and Nadia Wassef. 1999. Unfulfilled Promises. Women's Rights in Egypt. Population Council. http://www.popcouncil.org/pdfs/unfulfilled_promises.pdf

Levin, Yuval. 2000. American Aid to the Middle East: a Tragedy of Good Intentions. Institute. Institute for Advanced Strategic and Political Studies.

Moussa, Jasmine. 2006. The Reform of *Shari'a-* derived Divorce Legislation in Egypt: International Standards and the Cultural Debate. *University of Nottingham, Human Rights Law Commentary* 2.

Mustafa, Hala, Abd al-Ghaffar Shukor and Amre Hashem Rabi. 2005. Building Democracy in Egypt: Women's Political Participation, Political Party Life and Democratic elections. International Institute for Democracy and Electoral Assistance (IDEA) and the Arab NGO Network for Development (ANND).

Population Council. 2010. Survey Of Young People in Egypt: Preliminary Report. The Population Council Inc. http://www.popcouncil.org/pdfs/2010PGY_SYPEPrelimReport.pdf

Pratt, Nicola. 2001. Human Rights NGOs and the 'Foreign Funding Debate' in Egypt. Part of doctoral dissertation, entitled, "Globalization and the Postcolonial State: Human Rights NGOs and the Prospects for Democratic Governance in Egypt," funded by the Economic and Social Research Council, UK, 1998–2001.

Sharp, Jeremy M. 2011. Egypt in Transition. *Congressional Research Service*, (September), http://fpc.state.gov/documents/

organization/168035.pdf (accessed 30 September, 2011)

Theses consulted

Dandavati, Annie Gupta. 1992. The women's movement and the transition to democracy in Chile. PhD diss., University of Denver.

Dawood, Alia. 2010. Utilizing Mass Media in the Political Empowerment of Egyptian Women. PhD diss., University of Westminster in London.

Deejay, Aleksandar. 2011. Women's Social Change during Political Transformation in MENA: Egypt's Democratization Transition as a Case-Study. M.A. Work, the American University of Paris.

Eft, Natalie Darlene. 2011. Advocating for greater participation: feminisms in Egypt and the Muslim Brotherhood. M.A. Work, Georgetown University.

Mihindou, Piekielele Eugenia Tankiso. 2006. The African Renaissance and Gender: Finding the Feminist Voice. M.A. Work, University of Stellenbosch.

Osman, Hoda. 2003. Secular and Islamic Feminist voices in Egypt: Louder if together. M.A. Work, the American University in Cairo.

Raccagni, Michelle. 1982. Origins of feminism in Egypt and Tunisia. PhD diss., University of New York.

Sonneveld, Nadia. 2009. *Khul'* divorce in Egypt: public debates, judicial practices, and everyday life. PhD diss., University of Amsterdam.

Zantout, Mida R. 2006. *Khul'*: between Past and Present. M.A. Work, Institute of Islamic Studies McGill University.

Websites

Aman, Fatemeh. "Iran's vibrant feminist movement." *The feminist School Online*, 21 May 2009. http://feministschool.com/english/spip.php?article275 (accessed October 21, 2011)

Hoodfar, Homa. "The Women's Movement in Iran: Women at the Crossroads of Secularization and Islamization." *Iranian Chamber Society* (winter) 1999. http://www.iranchamber.com/society/articles/women_secularization_islamization5.php (accessed October 21, 2011)

Imbokodo. "Women's struggle in South Africa." South Africa History Online. http://www.sahistory.org.za/pages/governence-projects/womens-struggle/index.htm (accessed March 14, 2011)

iKNOWPolitics. "Egyptian Women organizations Coalition announced today." http://www.iknowpolitics.org/ar/node/41496 (accessed May 5, 2011)

Safe World for Women. "Constitutional Amendments exclude women Candidates from Presidential Elections." http://www.asafeworldforwomen.org/womens-rights/wr-egypt/589-statement-from-the-egyptian-centre-for-womens-rights.html (accessed April 5, 2011)

South African History online. "Women's struggle in South Africa." http://www.sahistory.org.za/pages/governence-projects/womens-struggle/struggle.htm (accessed March 18, 2011)

LIST OF APPENDIXES

Appendix I
Chronology of major events (January-August 2011) [73]

18/01/2011: Asmae Mahfouz, cofounder of the April 6 Youth Movement, posts a video blog on Facebook calling on Egyptians to demand their human rights and voice their disapproval of the regime of Hosni Mubarak. Following the Revolution, she became a prominent member of Egypt's Coalition of the Youth of the Revolution (Badran 2011).

25/01/2011: On National Police Day, the Egyptian revolution begins. Thousands of women from all different social classes, religions, age and affiliations go to the streets, participating actively in demonstrations.

28/01/2011: During the "The Friday of Anger," Sally Magdy Zahran is killed after thugs beat her on the head with bludgeons (El Wakil).

11/02/2011: President Hosni Mubarak steps down. On the same day, a South African journalist working for CBS News, Lara Logan, is assaulted in Midan Tahrir by several groups of men (60 Minutes).

17/02/2011: The Constitutional Committee is formed and it does not include any women (Spencer).

20/02/2011: Through a public statement, a coalition of women's NGOs refuses the illegitimate role of the National Council for Women in any formal representation of the Egyptian women (Nazra).

22/02/2011: Hundreds NGOs involved in women and development, legal studies and human rights announce the establishment of what they call "The Egyptian Coalition for Civic Education and Participation of Women" (Nabil).

25/02/2011: Sixty-three civil society organizations and institutions sign a statement in disapproval of the criteria and formation of the Constitutional Committee, whereby the committee does not include a single female expert (Rabbani).

02/03/2011: The "Egyptian Coalition for Civic Education and Women's Participation" revises the constitutional amendments. The coalition notices that Article 75, while stating that the Egyptian president cannot be married to a non-Egyptian woman, limits nominations to men only and suggested changing the sentence to say "shall not be married to a non-Egyptian" (Safe World for Women).

08/03/2011: Women's groups call for a "Millioneya March" to remind Egyptians of the role of women in the revolution but they are insulted and harassed by several groups of men who launched discriminatory slogans against women and women's involvement in politics (Naib).

09/03/2011: According to Amnesty International, a group of women arrested at a demonstration are threatened with prostitution charges and forced to submit to virginity checks by military authorities (Amnesty International).

19/03/2011: Egypt votes in a constitutional referendum for the amendment of eight articles of the 1971 Constitution (Michael).

23/03/2011: The Center for Women's Issues demonstrates in front of the Ministry of Justice following an attempt by the ministry to change the custody law, increasing fathers' visiting time from 3 hours per week to 48 hours (Ahmed).

30/03/2011: Article 38 of the Interim Constitution is announced, stating the following: "The law will govern the right of candidacy for the People's Assembly and *Shura* Council according to the determined electoral system, including a minimum the participation of women in both assemblies" but without specifying the exact number. This is the only law in the transition period that addresses the political participation of

185

women in society (Equality now).

-    Salafists protest to release Camilia, a Christian who converted to Islam and allegedly was being held in the church (Magdi).[74]

31/03/2011: Justice Tahani El-Gebali, vice president of the Supreme Constitutional Court, releases a statement on maintaining or abolishing the women's quota (Abdel Hamid Hafez).

01/04/2011 The ruling Supreme Council of the Armed Forces releases a decree amending seven articles in the penal code and enforcing harsher punishment in sexual harassment cases (Abdoun).

03/04/2011: TV anchor Bothaina Kamel states that she will run for president (Abdel Aziz).

04/04/2011: The Free Egyptian Party announces its inclusion of a women's program within its agenda, giving it an edge, according to an interview with Naguib Sawiris, who founded the party (Afify).

08/04/2011: During the Day of Cleansing, thousands of women, students and religious groups gather in Tahrir Square after the army drafted a draconian new law that banned protests and strike (Amar).

10/04/2011: A group of some sixteen women's organizations announce the launch of the Women's Organizations Coalition. The coalition's demands include a true representation of Egyptian women who participated in the revolution side by side with men and a major media's focus on women's activities. Some of the organizations participating in the coalition are the New Woman Foundation, Egyptian Women for a Better Society and Egyptian Women for Change (IKNOWPolitics).

11/04/2011: In front of the state television building, people who claim to be negatively affected by the custody law call for a march scheduled for May 5 to call for its amendment (Nasser).

-   According to Al Ahram Newspaper, the prime minister takes back his decision to name the national women's machinery a commission in response to the demands of women activists (Zaharan).

12/04/2011: A new law on political rights approved by the Supreme Council of the Armed Forces would deny Egyptian expatriates the right to vote, remove the quota for women in Parliament, adopt individual and proportional electoral lists and divide parliamentary elections into three phases (Othman).

13/04/2011: Suzanne Mubarak is under arrest (Repubblica).

15/04/2011: The prime minister meets with a group of women activists and leaders to discuss the fate and future of the National Council for Women. During the discussion a proposition is raised to establish a Ministry for Women's Affairs. Dr. Sharaf expresses his initial approval of this proposal (Rashwan).

17/04/2011: Naem Abu Ghadda, head of "si el Said" "the master" association, plans to establish a political party that will aim to recover men's strength and overthrow calls of liberation that were adopted by the former first lady and her affiliates to help women disobey their husbands under the pretext of "equality" (Abu Sakin).

-   The ECWR through a press release accuses the government of having appointed a number of governors without having appointing any women, a disregard to the principles of citizenship, justice and equality (ECWR).

18/04/2011: Ali Gomaa, the Grand *Mufti* of Al-Azhar, the oldest Islamic establishment in the region, promises to call for the amendment of the personal status law in regard to the custody of children by saying that he will announce a new *fatwa* that is fair to the fathers (Fahmy B.).

19/04/2011: Thousands of Salafis held a demonstration in front of the Ministry of Defense, calling for Egypt's military rulers to release a priest's wife who they say converted to Islam and is now being held by the Coptic Church. This demonstration is described as one of the largest that Salafis have organized in recent years (Egypt News Hub).

27/04/2011: Dozens of demonstrators assemble in front of the Press Syndicate in Cairo to demand the amendment of the Personal Status Laws, accusing former first lady Suzanne Mubarak of harming Egyptian families through the role she played in helping to pass the laws. Several new movements have organized the protests, such as the "Saving the Family" and "Egypt's Men Revolution" movements, and they included hundreds of fathers (Awadalla).

28/04/2011: Chancellor Mohamed Bakr announces the intention of the "Save the Egyptian Family" association, which is under construction, to file a lawsuit within a few days to abolish the National Council for Women and the National Council for Motherhood and Childhood on charges of corrupting the family (Fahmy B.; Abdel Hafiz).

29/04/2011: Nearly a thousand veiled Salafi women and their husbands demonstrate after Friday prayers to demand the resignation of Mufti Ali Gomaa and the appointment of new muftis by election (Ahramonline).

30/04/2011: Bothaina Kamel launches a new satellite channel (Kamel T) on the Egyptian satellite "Nile Sat," within the framework of her campaign (El Shourouq).

03/05/2011: Women activists welcomed the resolution of the minister of interior, Major General Mansour al-Issawi, to give Egyptian nationality to sons and daughters of Egyptian women married to Palestinians (Ali).

06/05/2011: Hundreds of veiled women and Salafis held a demonstration in front of Al-Azhar to denounce a fatwa of Mufti Ali Gomaa, who said that the *niqab* has nothing to do with religion (Al Bahery).

11/05/2011: Nehad Abul Komsan receives a death threat from the "northern region's enforcer for the religious discipline monitoring group" because of her statement opposing the cancellation of the law that gives the woman the right to initiate divorce, "*khul'* " (El Shamy).

13/05/2011: At least twelve people are killed in fighting that started Saturday in a Cairo suburb where, according to witnesses, Salafis had surrounded a church and demanded that those inside release Abeer Fakhry, a woman who supposedly converted to Islam. Islamist protesters have previously accused the Coptic Church of detaining two women, Camilia Shehata and Wafa Constantine, wives of Coptic priests (Al Masry Al Youm).

13/05/2011: Suzanne Mubarak enters jail.

15/05/2011: The Egyptian Coalition for Civil Education and Women's Participation during a roundtable meeting discusses the women's quota, saying that "the cancellation of the women's quota without alternative legal methods that guarantee women's political participation is pushing women back to square one" (ECWR).

17/05/2011: Mufti Ali Gomaa promises to establish a committee for the amendment of the Personal Status Laws in regard to the custody of children. Al-Azhar responds to the pressure of the Salafi trend and decides to form a committee to review the Personal Status Laws (Abdel Rahman).

18/05/2011: The Muslim Brotherhood's new "Freedom and Justice" political party's documents are submitted to the political parties committee. It includes lists of its founding members, its program, and bylaws. The list includes names of nine hundred women and ninety-three Copts (Fahmy and Elyan).

24/05/2011: Hundreds of fathers protest for custody laws in front of the Islamic Research Center. It entails calls by "Egyptian

Men's Revolution" (Thawret Regal Misr) and "Saving the Egyptian Family" (Inqaz AlUsra) movements to amend child custody and family laws to abide by Islamic *Shari'a* (Abdoun).

31/05/2011: A *Tagammu'* Party statement stresses that abolishing the allocation of a proportion of seats for women in Parliament as proposed by the bill is not the solution, but rather the adoption of the proposal that was previously presented by the party for an unconditional, open-list proportional system for the People's Assembly elections in which "the proportion of each gender is not less than 30 percent" (Misr el Gdida).

04/06/2011: AAW, the Association of International Civil Servants (AFICS), and the Coalition of Egyptian NGOs organize a convention in which a charter document is created to highlight civil society views on public issues, particularly those related to women, and give suggestions with regards to the new constitution (Khalil).

12/06/2011: The "Egyptian Men's Revolution" movement calls for a peaceful protest to pressure the government to take action to support the stability of Egyptian families. The movement demands the dissolution of the National Council for Women, amendments to the custody and family law, and the limitation of women's organizations (Magdi).

- Reem Abu Zeid announces the formation of the first women's party, called "The Egyptian Woman" party. The founder adds that the party will focus on the role of women in society with a special focus on marginalized women in slums (Salah).

20/06/2011: The Egyptian Islamic movement *Al-Jamaa Al-Islamiya*, through its political party El-Benaa wa El-Tanmia (Building and Development), argue that Suzanne Mubarak gave women too many rights, thus there should be a new balance in society. Calls for secularism are also met with flat refusal by the controversial Islamists (Tarek).

23/06/2011: A group of women form "A coalition of Women's Revolution" in Alexandria to empower women's political participation and increase their awareness. The campaign "Know Your Rights" will be launched on Friday to support the coalition's objectives (Samir).

28/06/2011: Three months after news surfaced that military police conducted virginity tests on female protesters, Samira Ibrahim, one of the victims, files an official complaint with military prosecution. Ibrahim gives military prosecutors a detailed account of her experience (Afify).

29/06/2011 Prime Minister Essam Sharaf meets with women and activists to discuss women's issues. He discusses means of women's inclusion in the coming period (Al Gali).

01/07/2011: The Muslim Sisterhood after sixty years prepares a conference. Muslim Brotherhood leaders and their wives attend this meeting (Elyan).

- The members of the National Council issue the "Constitutional Declaration Document." One of the suggestions is to achieve equality between women and men in the military service, in the police, and in the judiciary. It also suggests the establishment of a high commission against all forms of discrimination (Latif).
- The government initially agrees on two draft laws with two military decrees about the amendment of the laws related to the People's Assembly and *Shura* Council elections. The draft laws were submitted by the political and legislative groups to the Cabinet of Ministers. The amendments include granting a seat for women in the first half of the political parties' lists. The government says that this system would put women's representation at 20 percent at least (ECWR).

07/07/2011: A demonstration is held to demand a civil family law and the right for Egypt's Christians to divorce (Shukrallah).

- Political parties still refuse to place women on their election lists and allocate specific seats to women (ECWR).
- The Family Protection Coalition asks for the resignation of Justice Minister Abdel Aziz El-Gendy, believed to be postponing the process of revision of the Personal Status Laws. The Coalition intends to announce the Egyptian Family Charter by the end of July (ECWR).

17/07/2011: Women are not invited to consultations held by the prime minister regarding the formation of a new government in response to the demands of demonstrators in Tahrir Square. In the proposed government, only the name of one woman appears, Dr. Radwa Ashor, who is nominated for the position of culture minister (ECWR).

19/07/2011: Several Christians who demand the right to divorce and to remarry demonstrated in front of St. Mark Cathedral in Abbasseya. They are asking for the application of reimplementation of the 1938 regulation that gives nine reasons for divorce (Haitham al-Sharkawi).

24/07/2011: The Supreme Council of the Armed Forces releases a law on the amendments to the People's Assembly Law. This text cancels the women's quota system and states that each list of candidates must include at least one woman (David).

25/07/2011: Several NGOs refuse the Personal Status Law decree presented by the Family Appeal Court. The decree includes seven articles that call for the cancellation of *khul'*, custody of the mother to end when the male child reaches seven years old and the female child reaches ten years old, the father to have sole educational guardianship, reinforcement of the wife's obedience by coercive force in case the wife doesn't object to the warning in time, and cessation of alimony for the disobedient wife (Nazra).

27/07/2011: Judge Mohamed Atteya, minister of local development, announces that in their process of choosing new governors, he and Prime Minister Essam Sharaf are considering the nomination of women for the posts. A government source reveals the nomination of Judge Noha el Zeini, vice president of the administrative prosecution, among four other women, for the position of governor (Kamel).

30/07/2011: Egypt's local development minister says that Judge Noha el Zeini and the other women nominated have been excluded in a planned gubernatorial reshuffle (Al Masry Al Youm).

15/08/2011: Asmaa Mahfouz, also called the "Facebook girl," sits in front of an Egyptian military prosecutor Sunday to face charges of inciting violence against the military, insulting the SCAF, and spreading rumors. Even Hazem Salah Abu Ismail, an Islamist presidential candidate, condemned the arrest of Mahfouz (Fadel).

17/08/2011: The alliance of women's groups in Egypt sends a message to the government, asking for the inclusion of gender equality in the principles of the new constitution (Radio Sawa).

23/08/2011: During a meeting with representatives of women's groups, presidential candidate Amr Moussa emphasizes the need to develop a politically-neutral, national women machinery that is not affiliated with any party or with the government (Elhabbal).

08/09/2011: Meranda Moussa decides to establish a new political party to defend the rights of women and achieve social justice (Zaher).

15/10/2011: Following the creation of the Egyptian Women Charter, a coalition of five hundred NGOs establishes the Egyptian Women Union. The union is expected to provide technical support and establish linkages with women in neighboring countries in the region, and to mobilize five million women voters in the upcoming parliamentary and presidential elections, and the constitutional referendum. Hoda Badran, president of the AAW (Alliance for Arab Women), is elected as board chairwoman of the Union by acclamation (Shaalan).

20/12/2011: Some 4,000 women take to the streets in a march organized by the Mohamed ElBaradei Campaign and the April 6 Youth Movement. Women demonstrate peacefully and in unity against the violence of the ruling military council, and the assault of women in the streets by Egyptian soldiers (Carr 2011).

Final notes:
For a question of length and time constraints, this work only reported the events happened until August 2011. Therefore, it did not describe the demonstrations that happened in Tahrir Square in November 2011, as well as the results of the elections. The participation of ordinary women in both events has been exceptional. Women have participated in masses in the first free democratic parliamentary elections. The Muslim Brotherhood's (MB) political arm, the Freedom and Justice Party (FJP), secured 47.2% of lower house parliamentary seats, followed by

Al Nour party winning 24.7% of seats. At the time of writing this work three rounds of parliament elections had been completed where for the independent seats no women have won, and only 9 women won through their parties' lists (two women have been appointed by the SCAF to the 508 person body of the People Assembly, which means women comprise just 2% of the parliament). Furthermore, while discussing this work, the SCAF has ordered the reshuffle of the NCW, a decree that has been welcomed with very much criticism from the side of conservative forces.

Appendix II

<u>Groups and coalitions established after the revolution</u>

Facebook and online grouping

WOMEN OF EGYPT
Women of Egypt is a Facebook group administered by some young women and opened by Italian blogger Lucia Palmerini who, on the group's Facebook page, explains that women deserve more than what they have, and that they should fight for their rights and for their countries.

WOMEN OF EGYPT FOR DEMOCRACY
WED (Women of Egypt for Democracy) is an open online group supporting the empowerment of women in the changing political landscape of Egypt.

WORDS OF WOMEN FROM THE EGYPTIAN REVOLUTION
It is a group of independent filmmakers and activists who are working to document women's participation in the Egyptian Revolution. The goal of the group is that of reproducing women's participation. The filmmakers aspire to cover a variety of women from all spectrums of the Egyptian society and different regions in Egypt.

Groups

SAWA
It is an independent, non-affiliated Egyptian women's rights advocacy group. The mission is advocacy for the inclusion and engagement of women in rebuilding the nation. The activities of the group include media monitoring, encouraging more gender-sensitive media, raising awareness of women's issues, raising awareness of women's issues with fledgling political parties, and encouraging parties to put women on their agendas from the outset.

YOUNG FEMINIST MOVEMENT (YFM)
Formed in April 2011, the new Young Feminist Movement (YFM) is an advocacy group that seeks to influence decision makers, political parties and political movements by assuring proper gender balance, women's representation, and gender mainstreaming the parties' agendas. It stresses women's rights and highlights Egyptian women as part of the revolution without taking their needs out of the societal and political context in Egypt. The group is supported by Nazra for Feminist Studies.

EGYPTIAN WOMEN FOR DEMOCRACY AND AGAINST HARRASSMENT
Born as a Facebook group, the movement's aim is that of working to improve women's social standards, and doing advocacy on women's issues. It aims to build a constituency that will lobby for reforms in women's rights and the improvement of women's status. An advisory committee has been established which includes
experts in laws, education and health. The organization believes in listening to women's issues and empowering women. It aims to address the roots of gender problems and support legislations on a national level.

Coalitions

COALITION OF REVOLUTIONARY WOMEN

It is a coalition of independent Egyptian women and men who think that the revolution brought a backlash to women's rights in the country, in terms of political participation and representation. The coalition whose members are single individuals or experts from NGOs and CSOs organized seminars, workshops and conferences to debate the current situation of women in the post-revolutionary Egypt.

The goals of the coalition are:

*Pressure decision makers for the participation of Egyptian women in decision-making positions in government and the various committees.

*The definition of the role played by Egyptian women before, during, and after the revolution.

*Highlight the contributions of women in the Egyptian revolution.

*Pressure the relevant committees for amendments of enacted legislation in order for women to acquire their rights, for example: the law on political rights and the principle of equality between men and women in the formation of the new parliament, constitution, etc.

*Maintain the gains of Egyptian women in legal, social, and economic matters.

COALITION FOR CIVIC EDUCATION AND WOMEN'S PARTICIPATION

This coalition, created after the revolution, includes around 269 NGOs involved in women and development, legal studies, and human rights. The coalition wants to unify efforts in spreading awareness on democratization in Egypt following the events of January 25. The Egyptian Coalition underlines the importance of women's role in achieving social and political change and points to the geographic diversity of the civil associations participating in the coalition, enabling them to spread the principles of education, civic culture, and women's rights.

The coalition aims to activate the role of civil society and youth in voluntary work and the participation of women in all the stages of democratic transition.

EGYPTIAN WOMEN UNION

The Egyptian Women Union, established on October 15, comprises 500 NGOs. Hoda Badran, secretary-general of the Alliance for Arab Women, is the current chairperson of the union. Four other NGOs were included as members of the executive committee. The union is expected to provide technical support and establish linkages with women in neighboring countries in the region. It is expected to mobilize five million women voters in the upcoming parliamentary and presidential elections, and the constitutional referendum. Having the eradication of illiteracy among its priorities, the union will engage in a national project for illiteracy irradication in the coming year or two.

INDEPENDENT COALITION OF WOMEN NGOs

This coalition includes fifteen established NGOs that mainly focus on women's rights under the Constitution in the transitional period. The coalition refuses the illegitimate role of the National Council of Women and its representation of Egyptian women calling for its dissolution.

UNION OF PEASANTS WOMEN

Female peasant workers have established in Imbaba district's Werdan village the first union for women farmers in Egypt at the end of October. The union aims at defending women's rights within the sector and ensuring equal treatment between women peasants and their male counterparts.

Women Parties

THE NEW WOMAN PARTY

The New Woman party was formed by Reem Abu Eid after the revolution of January 25. The party aims to combat discrimination against women in the current transition. The party welcomes the accession of any woman and men of any ideology. The party aims to review laws that harm women issued under the former regime, and to protect women from any form of violence, and to support rural women and marginalized groups, promoting education and the eradication of illiteracy. The party also takes a distance from women's groups which, according to the founder, have not benefitted women at all.

[]

EGYPTIAN WOMEN

Egyptian Women is a new party that aims at achieving social justice for Egyptian women. The party's main goals revolve around four axes: political, developmental, social, and cultural. The party aims to establish sustainable development projects in various fields such as health, education, and agriculture. The Egyptian Women Party is still under formation, but it has been welcomed by many prominent Egyptian women

Appendix III
EGYPTIAN WOMEN'S CHARTER

EGYPTIAN WOMEN: PARTNERS IN THE REVOLUTION AND IN BUILDING DEMOCRATIC EGYPT.

Egyptian women constitute half of Egypt. They have been active in January 25th revolution and side by side with men, they demonstrated in main squares of Egypt, they spent the nights on streets to make sure that the revolution will not be hijacked or stopped, they nursed the wounded, lamented the dead, chanted and danced when they became victorious and also cleaned the aftermath when they withheld the demonstrations. They in brief, have put an end to the corrupt regime and to the dictatorship. They are still active in translating the slogans of the revolution: freedom, dignity and social justice to a reality in every Egyptian citizen's life. They are still participating in all Friday's demonstrations in public squares confirming that democracy that they and men promised Egypt to achieve will be fulfilled soon. They want to see the themes of the revolution Freedom, Dignity and Social Justice opening new opportunities for them to obtain equality and justice.

Egyptian women have agreed that the following are their demands:

First: Representation of women

Women should be represented in the committee that will be entrusted with drafting the constitution. Such representation should take into consideration their size in the population and their past, present and future role in building the society.
Women should also be participants in all legislative committees and in all dialogue forums that discuss national issues.
Women should occupy at least 40 percent of the ministerial positions and should be in decision making positions, in political parties electoral lists.
The new constitution should spell out clearly full equality between man and women in all spheres of life and the elimination of all sorts of discrimination against them.
The parliamentary elections should be run through proportional electoral lists which have at least 30% women
Selection for leadership posts and all positions should be based on qualifications and objective professional requirements with no discrimination.

Second: International Conventions

The Egyptian government should hold its commitment to all international human rights conventions including the convention on the Elimination of all forms of Discrimination against women.

Egyptian representation in International human rights committees should include women from government and non-government organizations

Third: Social and Economic Rights.

Egyptian women particularly the poor should have access to basic services to enable them to combine their roles at home and in society.

It is a shame that 40 percent of Egyptian women are still illiterate in the age of information and technology. Without the use of technology the 25th revolution would not have succeeded

Only 16% of Egyptian full time workers are female. In the current times of insecurity a preference can be observed to first support men as the "traditional breadwinners" in getting out of unemployment. Therefore now even greater efforts are needed to support women claiming their economic rights. Women should have equal opportunities in accessing the labor market, credit, capital and skills training. At the work place women should enjoy decent working conditions, prospects for advancement as well as protection from any kind of sexual harassment.

Fourth: Legislation

All discriminatory legislation against women should be reviewed and redressed on basis of equality and justice. The Family Law in particular needs to be reformed to reflect human dignity and justice for all members of the family and protect the children

Fifth: Women and judiciary posts

Women graduates of law schools should have equal opportunity to acquire judiciary posts and climb the ladder up to being judges and in all branches and ranks of the system.

Sixth: National Women Machinery

Egyptian women demand a strong national women machinery along with other mechanisms like gender focal points in all ministries and governorates, Gender equality committee inside the parliament and an Ombudsperson for gender equality to ensure gender mainstreaming in all policies, plans and programs of the government, of the legislative and judiciary systems.

Seventh: Media:

A national policy should be formulated to reflect a positive image of women and to help create a culture with no discrimination against women.

Appendix IV
List of interviewed experts

1. FATEMA KHAFAGY (19/06/2011)
Fatema Khafagy is a women's rights activist and policy expert on women's rights. She established and presided over the first ombudsperson office on gender equality in Egypt. Dr. Khafagy is a board member of the Alliance for Arab Women and the Centre for Egyptian Women Legal Assistance (CEWLA).

2. MARIZ TADROS (19/06/2011)
Mariz Tadros is a research fellow at the Institute of Development Studies (IDS), a participant in the Pathways of Women's Empowerment Research Programme Consortium, a former assistant professor of political science at the American University in Cairo, and a journalist for Al-Ahram Weekly.

3. DALIA ZIADA (20/06/2011)
Dalia Ziada is an Egyptian rights activist and blogger honored by Newsweek as one of 150 most influential women

in the world, selected by the Daily Beast as one of world's seventeen bravest bloggers, and named by Time Magazine as rights champion. She found the American Islamic Congress in Egypt and manages AIC activities in the MENA region.

4. AFEF EL SAEED (20/06/2011)

Afef El Saeed is the executive director of the *Heya* Foundation for Women to stop discrimination and violence against women. She is a prominent activist and writer and utilizes arts and culture to build awareness.

5. MYRIAM ZAKI (22/06/2011)

Myriam Zaki is a television show host and presenter. Her prominent shows have been "Together- ma3an"and "Beladab" and "Sout bent Masr" to empower women and young girls.

6. HAMDY EL HENNAWI (25/06/2011)

Hamdy El Hennawi has worked in the area of population and development for fourty years and considers the upgrade of women's position in the society as a basic developmental factor. He studies the national costs of divorce and violence against women. He also defended his daughter, who was the first woman to ask publicly for a DNA test to recognize the paternity of her daughter, born from an unofficial marriage.

7. ABDEL RAHMAN AYYASH (25/06/2011)

Abdel Rahman Ayyash is an independent Islamist blogger who writes for *Al-Ghareeb* (The Stranger). A former member of the Muslim Brotherhood, he now considers himself a liberal Islamist.

8. SARAH MOHAMMED (25/06/2011)

Sarah Mohammed is one of the youngest members of the

Muslim Brotherhood. Daughter of one of the leaders of the Muslim Brothers, she became a political activist at a very young age. She is pushing for a stronger and leading position for women in the movement.

9. DINA WAHBA (26/06/2011)
Dina Wahba is a women's rights activist and coordinator of the women's committee in the newly established Egyptians Democratic Social Party.

10. M. S. (Assistant of the mufti) (24/06/2011)

11. IMEN BIBARS (03/07/2011)
Imen Bibars is a social entrepreneur, and co-founder and current chair of the Association for the Development and Enhancement of Women, a CSO providing credit and legal aid for impoverished women heading their households.

12. FATEMA EMAM (05/07/2011)
Fatema Emam is an Islamic feminist and activist working on women's rights. She is also a lead researcher at Nazra Feminist Studies.

13. DINA ABOU EL SOUD (06/07/2011)
Dina Abou El Soud is a young activist and a founding member of the "Coalition of Revolutionary Women." After the revolution, she became particularly active in the field of women's rights.

14. HODA BADRAN (06/07/2011)
Hoda Badran is chairperson of The Alliance for Arab Women and the founder and director of Arab Women's Solidarity Association.

15. BOTHAINA KAMEL (10/07/2011)
Bothaina Kamel is an anchorwoman and a cofounder of We Are Watching You, an election monitoring group set up to

observe parliamentary elections, she is the first woman in the history of Egypt to run for president.

16. KHALED HAMZA (12/07/2011)

Khaled Hamza is the editor of the Muslim Brotherhood's official website. Hamza is considered a leading voice of moderation within the party and is central to its youth outreach efforts. In a crackdown on the Brotherhood during the run-up to elections in 2008, Hamza was jailed for several weeks.

17. AZZA KAMEL (13/07/2011)

Azza Kamel is the director of Appropriate Communication Techniques for Development (ACT) and the founder of the Women Research Centre. Ms. Kamel, over the past sixteen years, has worked as a women's rights activist to fight violence against women by advocating equality between men and women.

18. ALIA DAWOOD (17/07/2011)

Alia Dawood holds a PhD from the School of Media, Arts and Design at the University of Westminster in London. Her PhD work was entitled Utilizing Mass Media in the Political Empowerment of Egyptian Women. He research interest is Arab women and media.

19. MOHASEN SABER (22/07/2011)

Mohasen Saber is the director of Radio *Motallaqat,* dedicated to women whose marriages have failed and who were up against tremendous legal odds.

20. FARIDA NAQASH (23/07/2011)

Farida Naqash is the editor-in-chief of *Al Ahali* newspaper and a founding member of the progressive *Tagammu* party. She is also a member and founder of the NGOs Forum for Women's Development. This forum is a women's organization that works to abolish all forms of discrimination against women.

21. DOAA ABDELAAL (24/07/2011)

Doaa Abdelaal is a council member of the international solidarity network Women Living under Muslim Laws, in which where she participates in different regional plans for supporting and advocating women's rights. Since April 2010, she has worked as MENA Regional Coordinator and Arabic Facilitator for the iKnow Politics Project.

22. NEHAD ABOL KOMSAN (26/07/2011)

Nehad Abol Komsan is a lawyer and the chair of the Egyptian Center for Women's Rights, an organization founded in 1996 that promotes the involvement of women in political and public life. She is also a member of the Supreme Council of Islamic Affairs.

Appendix V
Topics discussed during the semi-structured interviews

- The participation of women in the revolution
- Women's political and constitutional rights and recent political developments concerning women's activism in the transitional phase
- Representation of women in leading positions like the presidency and/or ministries
- The issue of a quota for women in Parliament
- March 8, International Women's Day
- The military council and its relationship with the women's movement
- The feminist movement in Egypt
- Reforms of the Personal Status Laws
- Religious conservative groups and their interpretations of women's rights
- Social visions on women's political roles and rights

Appendix VI

Survey results & figures

Q1: Gender of the respondents

claudia ruta

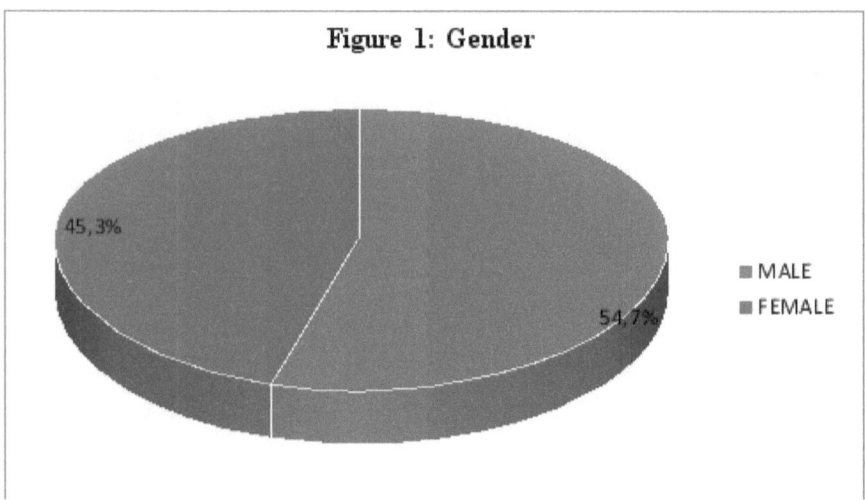

Figure 1: Gender

Q2: Age

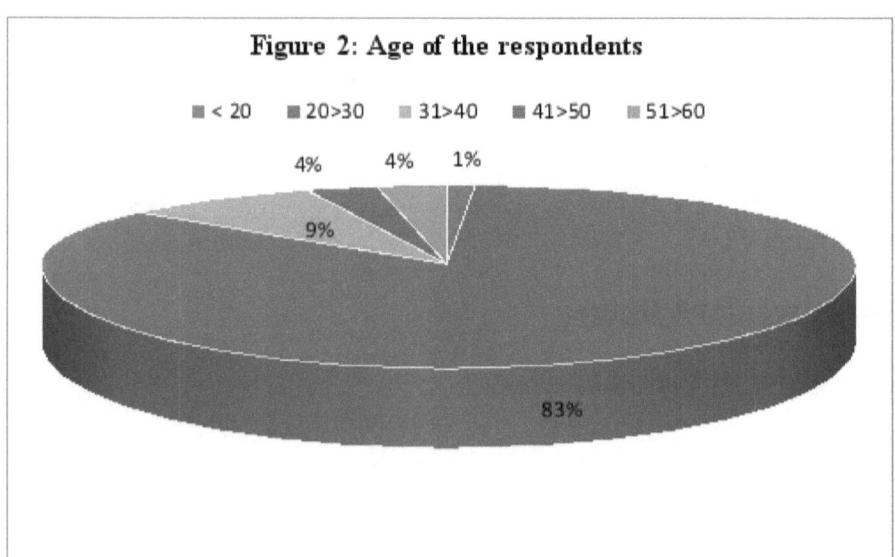

Figure 2: Age of the respondents

Q3: Political orientation

Figure 3: Political Orientation

65.9

19.6

5.1

11.6

| Liberal | Conservative | Moderate | Other |

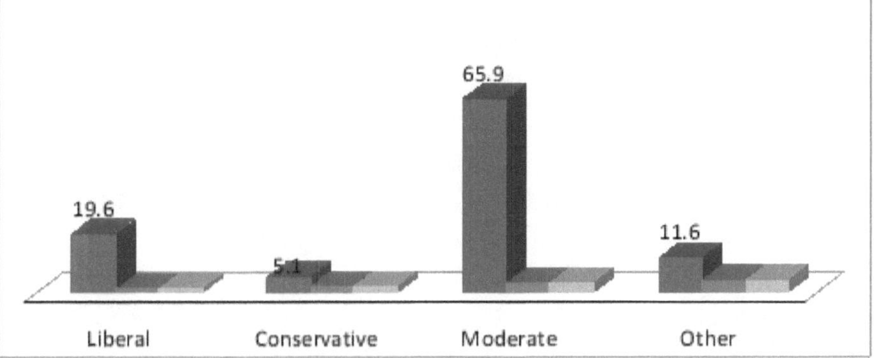

Figure 4: Political orientation males vs females

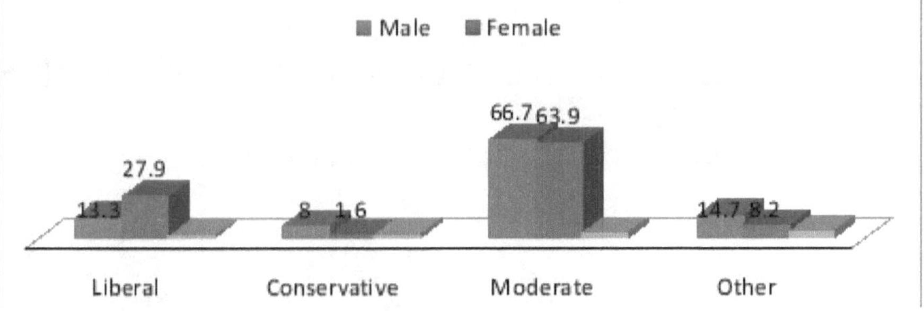

■ Male   ■ Female

66.7 63.9

27.9

13.3

8 1.6

14.7 8.2

| Liberal | Conservative | Moderate | Other |

Q4: Education degree

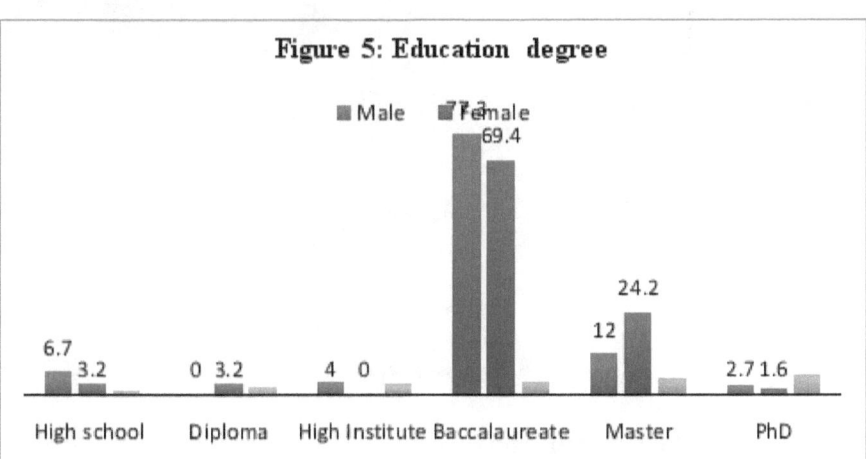

Figure 5: Education degree

■ Male   ■ Female

77.3
69.4

24.2

12

6.7
3.2

0 3.2

4 0

2.7 1.6

| High school | Diploma | High Institute | Baccalaureate | Master | PhD |

Q5: Demographics (129 answers)

City	Number
Cairo	97
Alexandria	2
Port Said	1
Qena	1
Banha	4
Zagazig	1
Giza	14
Shibin El Kom	1
Tanta	1
Other	7

Q6: What do you think about women's participation in the January 25 revolution?

Figure 6: Women's participation in the revolution

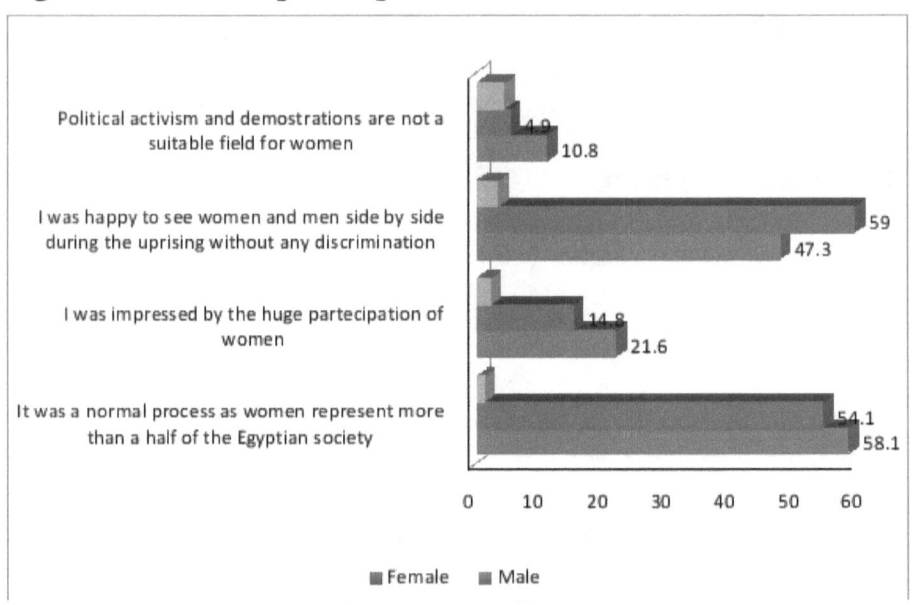

Q7: Please indicate to what extent you agree with the following statements:

"Egyptian feminist groups…"

	1	2	3	4	5	Rating Average	Response count
The feminist movement asserts that women are better than men	5,2 % (6)	9,5 % (11)	15,5 % (18)	41,4 % (48)	28,4 % (33)	3,78	116
The feminist movement supports the rights of women and calls for gender equality	24,1 % (28)	36,2 % (42)	20,7 % (24)	16,4 % (19)	2,6 % (3)	2,37	116
Groups that articulate a Western agenda	32,4 % (36)	39,6 % (44)	11,7 % (13)	7,2 % (8)	9,0 % (10)	3,88	111
Groups formed by members of the upper class only	20,2 % (23)	34,2 % (39)	18,4 % (21)	9,6 % (11)	17,5 % (20)	3,38	114
Groups formed by members belonging to different classes	0,9 % (1)	14,4 % (16)	18,0 % (20)	38,7 % (43)	27,9 % (31)	2,55	111
Groups formed by members with a secular political view	22,2 % (26)	22,2 % (26)	21,6 % (25)	12,9 % (15)	20,7 % (24)	3,69	116
Groups formed by members with different political orientations	15,0 % (17)	12,4 % (14)	17,7 % (20)	52,2 % (59)	2,7 % (3)	2,35	113

1: Strongly agree;   2: Agree;   3: Neutral;   4: Disagree;   5: Strongly disagree

"On March 8, during International Women's Movement Q8: Day, activists for women's rights went to Tahrir Square to celebrate the event and present their demands, but they faced verbal and physical harassment."

Please indicate to what extent you agree with the following statements:

	1	2	3	4	5	Rating Average	Response count
It was the right place and time for women to present their demands	14,3 % (16)	21,4 % (24)	14,3 % (16)	34,8 % (39)	15,2 % (17)	3,15	112
It was not the suitable time to talk about women's rights	12,5 % (15)	35,0 % (42)	15,0 % (18)	22,5 % (27)	15, % (18)	2,93	120
There was no need to demonstrate as	7,0 % (8)	13,9 % (16)	15,7 % (18)	37,4 % (43)	26,1 % (30)	3,62	115

	1	2	3	4	5		
women in Egypt already have all their rights							
I was disappointed in what women activists faced on March 8 as I thought that the revolution brought acceptance toward women's political participation	33,0 % (38)	40,9% (47)	12,2% (14)	10,4% (12)	3,5 % (4)	2,10	115

1: Strongly agree; 2: Agree; 3: Neutral; 4: Disagree; 5: Strongly disagree

Q9: "After the revolution, we noted a scarce representation of women in key decision-making positions like in the Constitutional Committee, as heads of governorates, and in the ministries, in which just one woman was appointed as minister." Please indicate to what extent you agree with the following statements:

	1	2	3	4	5	Rating Average	Response count
I was disappointed to see such a scarce representation of women, especially after their strong participation in the revolution	19,3 % (21)	26,6 % (29)	30,3% (33)	20,2% (22)	3,7 % (4)	2,62	109
A very small number of women in Egypt have the expertise to cover these positions	10,3 % (12)	31,9 % (37)	12,1 % (12)	26,7 % (31)	19,0% (22)	3,12	116
Politics is for men only and women should not be involved in politics or in positions of responsibility	5,4 % (6)	5,4 % (6)	8,0 % (9)	33,0% (37)	48,2% (54)	4,13	112
This was not done on purpose by the government	3,5 % (4)	35,4% (40)	27,4% (31)	25,7% (29)	8,0 % (9)	2,99	113
This is not a real problem in the transitional phase	10,5% (12)	36,8% (42)	17,5% (20)	25,4% (29)	9,6 % (11)	2,87	114
After the transitional phase, the percentage of women in key decision-making positions will increase	11,5 % (13)	40,7 % (46)	24,8% (28)	16,8% (19)	6,2 % (7)	2,65	113

1: Strongly agree; 2: Agree; 3: Neutral; 4: Disagree; 5: Strongly disagree

Q10: What do you think about a quota (a fixed number of seats)

for women in Parliament?

Figure 7: On the quota

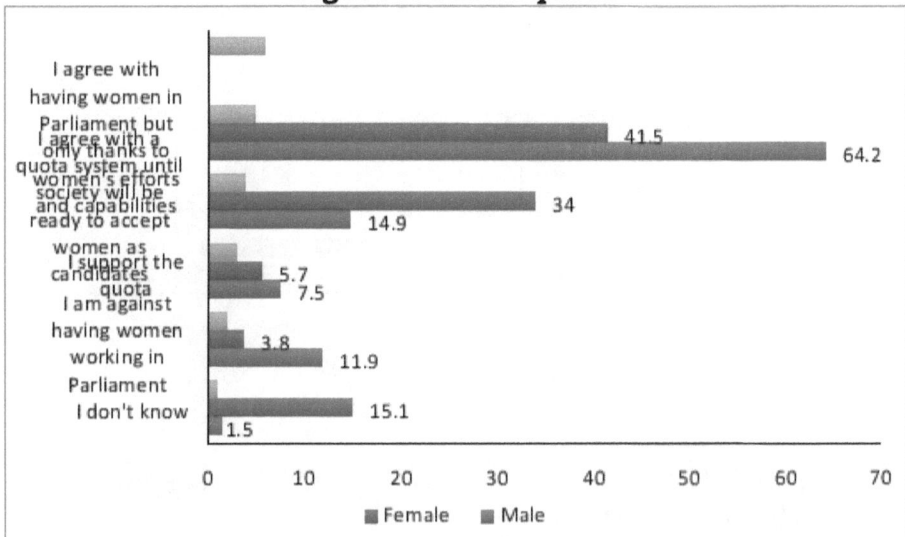

Q11: Do you agree with the ideas of women holding key political positions like the presidency?

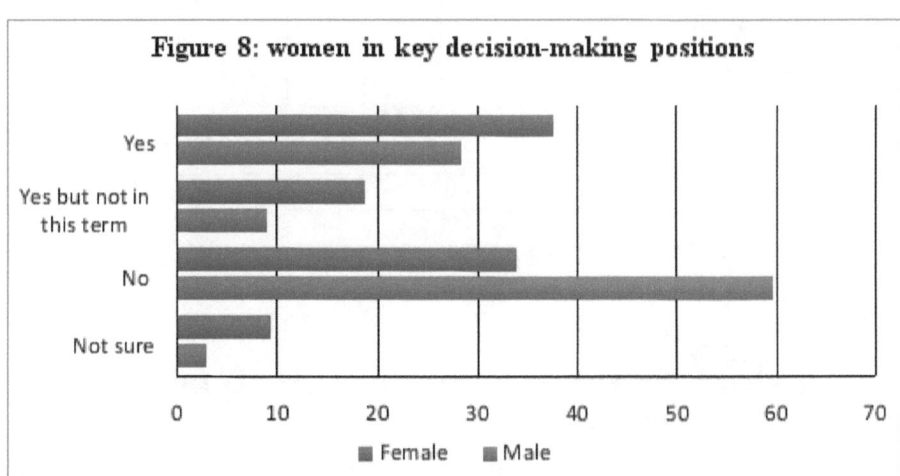

Q12: Do you agree with the law of khul' in its current form?

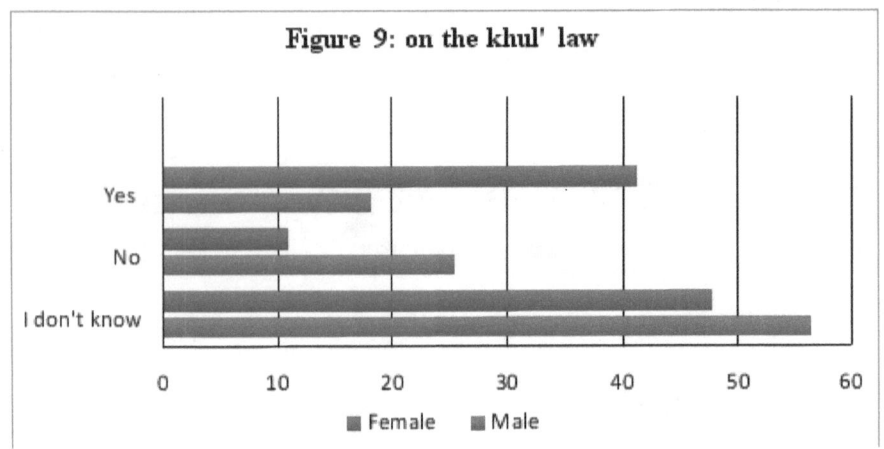

Figure 9: on the khul' law

Q13: For those who answered no, please specify for which reasons (Open question)
Q14: Do you agree with the Custody Law in its current form?

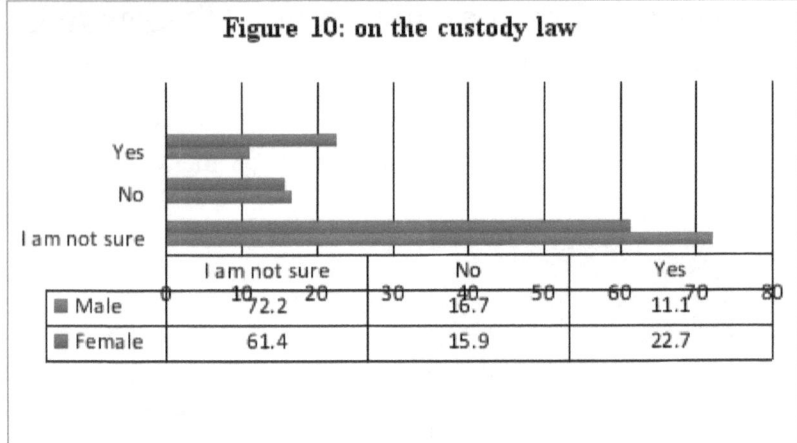

Figure 10: on the custody law

	I am not sure	No	Yes
■ Male	72.2	16.7	11.1
■ Female	61.4	15.9	22.7

Q15: For those who answered no, please specify for which reasons (Open question)

Q16: Do you agree on maintaining the age of marriage for girls at 18 instead of 16?

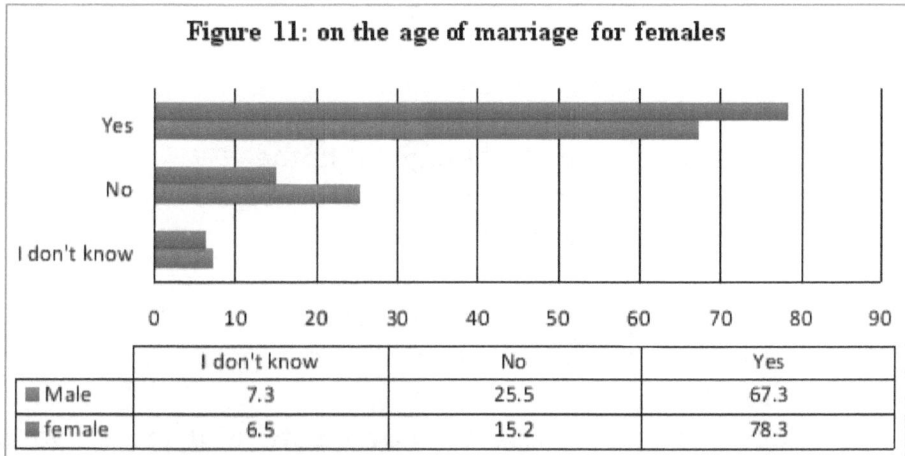

Figure 11: on the age of marriage for females

	I don't know	No	Yes
■ Male	7.3	25.5	67.3
■ female	6.5	15.2	78.3

Q17: For those who answered no, please specify for which reasons (Open question)
Q18: Are you with the idea of having religious leadership in post-Mubarak Egypt?

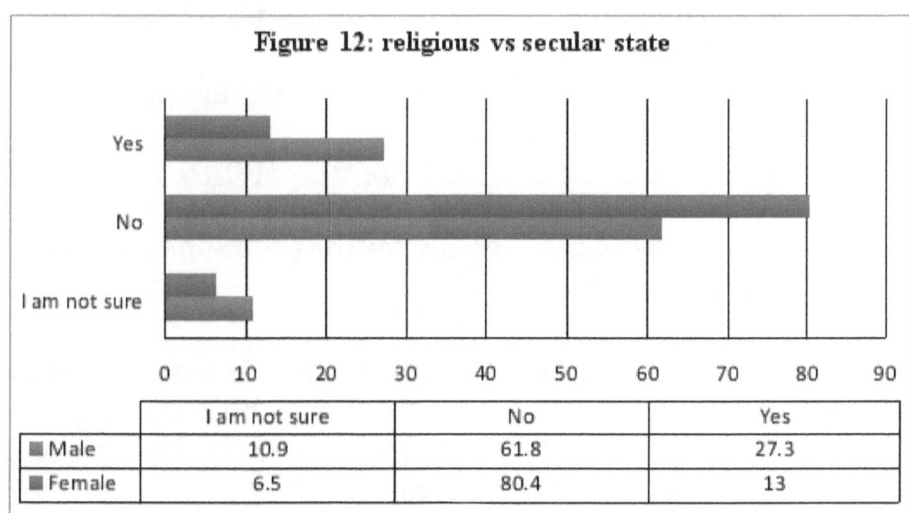

Figure 12: religious vs secular state

	I am not sure	No	Yes
■ Male	10.9	61.8	27.3
■ Female	6.5	80.4	13

Q19: What are the main difficulties that, in your opinion,
[75]women face in Egypt? (Open answer)
- Conservative Islam, which puts women in an inferior position
- Male oriented society and masculinity

- Lack of social assistance in case of widowhood and divorce
- Sexual harassment
- Scarce education in rural areas
- Unequal social roles taught at home
- Economic stagnancy and difficulty for women and men in getting married
- Poverty
- Discrimination in the field of work
- Discrimination in political participation and in the legal system
- Lack of awareness for women in rural areas about their civil and social rights which are guarantee by law and religion
- Lack of strong organizations to monitor and activate the laws that protect women and their rights
- Egyptian women are treated as inferior and less capable than men so they face social, political and economic inequality
- Lack of genuine religiosity among the Egyptians
- Domestic violence
- Lack of social trust in women's capabilities

Q20: Who do you hold responsible for the problems women [76]face in Egypt? (Open answer)

- Egyptian families that fail to educate women and to install a culture of equality among children
- Schools that fail to develop women's self-esteem and the deterioration of education
- Media that portray women as sexual objects and encourage this behavior
- Religious conservatism
- The government, which creates unemployment and political insecurity
- Women themselves, when they do not ask for their

rights even when they know that they are abused
- Discriminatory laws against women

Q21: Which social and political roles do you think women should have after the revolution? (Open answer)

- Women have a pivotal role in bringing up a new and bright generation of young people
- The same as before the revolution
- Equal roles in all areas
- Leadership of true Egyptian women respectful of true religious and social values
- Raise children and work in areas where sexual divisions are respected
- Effective participation in making decisions
- Education roles, especially at home
- Start with developing themselves and their abilities to cope with the needs and the requirements of the new period, educate themselves, and know the rights guaranteed to them by religion and laws
- Start to participate in the political process by joining the parties that are compatible with their thoughts, ideologies, and political points of view
- They should be allowed to work in any field
- Women should be involved in all areas of political and social life. There should be no difference whatsoever between women's participation compared to that of men
- Women that know their rights must be teachers to those who don't know
- Positive participation in parties and CSOs
- All feminists and women's groups must be united together to change the laws, raise awareness of social roles, work to spread political awareness among women, encourage women to have access to the ballot box and have a free and conscious choice, help

women participate in new parties, and train women politically to be able to be candidates
- Women's groups must pay attention to social problems related to children, ignorance, and poverty

---

[1] In Egypt a unified women or feminist movement has never existed. Differences have always persisted between secular and Islamist women, as well as women of different generations. Today the majority of the Egyptian feminists, pseudo-feminists, and activists are also members of civil-society organizations (CSOs) and non-governmental organizations (NGOs), making their activities mixed between a developmental approach based on social activism and a political orientation. For women activists I refer to Karam's definition of those "women that use a secular approach in articulating discourses on and of women, on a broad socio-political level" (Karam 1998, 4). Even though the term feminism has been often refused for its Western connotations and both cultural and political criticisms have been directed at it, feminist or pseudo-feminist groups in Egypt are still moved by "individual or collective awareness that women have been and continue to be oppressed in diverse ways and for diverse reasons, [attempting] towards liberation from this oppression involving a more equitable society with improved relations between women and men" (Ibid., 5). Those women that I interviewed for this work label themselves in different ways as belonging to the *al-haraka al-nissa'iyya* (the women's movement) and *al-haraka al-nassa'wiyya* (the feminist movement). Some women, even though they possess a feminist ideology, reject the term *al-haraka al-nassa'wiyya,* which seems to be discriminatory and related exclusively to women's problems. In this work I have specifically focused on secular-oriented activists who are those who advocate a separation between religion and politics, which does not necessarily denote anti-religious or anti-Islamic positions. Other forms of Arab feminism, namely Muslim and Islamic feminism, will not be considered in detail in this work. Moreover, this work does not want to generalize but also considering those groups and civil society organizations' activities related to women's political empowerment. Therefore, the work does not address issues related for example to female genital mutilation (FGM) or sexual harassment, a field to which, undoubtedly civil society organizations bring important support.

[2] A period of transition is the interval between one political system and another which usually results in the replacement of those currently in power. Transitions from authoritarian rule of the South American and Eastern European states are typical of all transitions.

[3] Patriarchy is defined as a hierarchy of authority that is controlled and dominated by males in which women's roles are subordinate to the role of the father (Knauss 1987, xii).

[4] With the concept of hegemonic power, Gramsci describes the way in which relations of power work, both during ordinary times and during times of transition. With the idea of hegemony, Gramsci explores the interplay of coercion

and consent which forms the dynamic of relations of power (Karam 1998, 24). Hegemony does not mean violence but it means ascendancy achieved through culture, institutions, and persuasion (Lorber 2010, 218). Gramsci explains that in order to fight this, there must be a politically strong struggle that involves a process of negotiation, concession, and underlying threat. This view of power is derived principally from the works of Antonio Gramsci and Michel Foucault. See Antonio Gramsci, *Selections from the Prison Notebooks*, and Michel Foucault *Power/Knowledge*.

[5] The discipline of international relations (IR) has been particularly reluctant to acknowledge feminist studies. However, as with other disciplines, feminists have been infiltrating and transforming the theory/practice of IR (Peterson 1998, 581). Feminist theories argue that international politics can be fully understood only by introducing gender study to the analysis of global politics; they describe women's invisibility and gender subordination in the theory and practice of IR. Feminist scholars like Peterson and Runyan advise on the importance of adopting gender lenses to investigate international politics (Dunne, Kurki and Smith 2007, 186).

[6] The content of the interviews carried out with the experts have been presented in the third chapter and in some occasions also in the second chapter.

[7] Using this research technique, the first respondents on the basis of suggestions helped me to identify other people who might qualify for inclusion in the research.

[8] Table 1 gives an overview of the interviewed and their social attributes.

[9] This kind of research has been time-consuming. Qualitative information is sometimes difficult to be analyzed as it requires a long time to transcribe interviews.

[10] Focus group topics are presented in the appendix n. 6.

[11] All participants shared with me their personal stories and feelings about their participation in the revolution. However, the analysis has been conducted only on issues considered relevant to the goals of this research, regrettably ignoring some parts of the collected ethnographic data.

[12] These countries have been selected not only for the similarities and differences of their political processes but also because of a personal interest and knowledge in the cases selected.

[13] The African National Congress (ANC) founded in 1912 was the most important leftist party in South Africa during the struggle against apartheid. Early in 1943, women were granted full membership within the ANC with the right to vote and to participate actively at all levels. A Woman Commission was also created. In the post-apartheid period, it remained the major political party of the country. For the first half of the twentieth century, women were engaged in political struggles, but their roles remained that of auxiliaries with no voting rights within the ANC. Only in 1943 did they become full members, but when the women's league of the ANC was developed, it maintained its auxiliary status (Hassim 2006, 22).

[14] A previous charter was developed in 1954. This first charter identified women's demands within the context of the national liberation movement.

[15] Dr. Sonia Alvarez distinguishes between *feministas/autónomas,* those who remain autonomous from party structures, and the *políticas/militants* with a policy of double militancy (concurrent participation in feminist and party/revolutionary organizations). Sonia Alvarez in "Pathways for Women in Democratic Transitions: International Experiences and lessons learned" (UN Women Conference, June 2, 2011).

[16] Before al-Ghazali, Labiba Ahmed founded the Society of Egyptian Ladies' Awakening in late 1920. She pushed for a combination of Islam and nationalism. Her aim was to introduce the image of the "new Islamic woman" as credible alternative to the "new secular woman". Zeinab became one of the hers of Labiba (Baron 2005, 189-190).

[17] Egypt instated reservations to Articles 2, 9, 16, and 29. According to its reservation to Article 16, which recognizes equality between men and women in family matters and equal rights in marriage's dissolution, Egypt stated that "respect for the sacrosanct nature of the firm religious beliefs that govern marital relation in Egypt may not be called into question."

[18] According to Decree-Law No.44, the husband's remarrying without the first wife consent should be considered harmful and the wife should be granted divorce automatically (Bernard-Maugiron, 2008).

[19] In 1994, the UN International Conference on Population and Development (ICPD) convened in Cairo. The conference addressed taboo topics like abortion, violence, and reproductive rights, as well as issues of common concern, like the equality before the law. A new generation of Islamist women started to stress Islam's compatibility with UN-stipulated standards of women's rights and point to patriarchal traditions as being responsible for the discrimination against women (Guenena and Wassef 1999, 48-49).

[20] In 2004, a new family court was established to mainstream family cases and a new nationality law allowed the children of Egyptian women with non-Egyptian spouses to gain nationality.

[21] Law No.4 of 2005 set the period of child custody for both boys and girls with the mother until the age of fifteen. A divorced woman has the right to live in the marital home with the children until the time of *hadāna* ends, or the husband should provide her with another place to stay with her children. However, if she remarries, she loses the custody of the children (Bernard-Maugiron 2010, 22).

[22] Interview with Hoda Badran, 06/07/2011.

[23] Interview with Imen Bibars, 03/07/2011.

[24] Interview with Farida Naqash, 23/07/2011.

[23] The women referred to in this work are all activists in the sense that they are actively involved in articulating discourses on and of women on a broad

socio-political level. The difficulty arises in trying to clarify the fine lines between social activism, political involvement, and feminism, as the three are sometimes interrelated. When I want to generalize, I call them women activists, without underlying to what degree they consider themselves feminists or pseudo-feminists.

[25] *Kefaya,* meaning "enough," is an Egyptian movement composed of intellectuals, NGOs, human rights activists, women's groups, and Muslims and Christians alike, including different ideological orientations such as nationalists, Nasserists, communists, liberals, and even Islamists. Announced in 2004, *Kefaya* gained prominence during the September 2005 presidential elections, which Mubarak won by a landslide. Even though the *Kefaya* movement failed to stir mass protests and expand beyond the middle-class elite, it represents the first democratic movement of protest that succeeded to combine different ideological fronts.

[26] The Emergency Law gave the security forces power of arrest, detention, torture and abuse of human rights, and restriction of demonstrations. The law was imposed during the 1967 Arab-Israeli war and re-imposed after the assassination of Sadat.

[27] Interview with Afef El Saeed, 20/06/2011.

[28] Interview with Dalia Ziada, 20/06/2011.

[29] Interview with Fatema Khafagy, 19/06/2011.

[30] Interview with Ayyash Abdel Rahman, 25/06/2011.

[31] Interview with Hamdy El Hennawi, 25/06/2011.

[32] Interview with Dina Wahba, 26/06/2011.

[33] The fact that official sexual assaults have not been reported does not mean that they did not happen. However, it has been estimated by civil society organizations working in the field of violence against women that in the days of the revolution, this kind of crime was remarkably reduced.

[34] The SCAF has adopted amendments to existing electoral laws that may benefit individual candidates, enabling former members of the now-disbanded NDP to re-enter political life (Sharp 6, 2011).

[35] Only the feminist Nawal El Saadawi tried to run for the presidency in 2005, but she withdrew from the ballot.

[36] Interview with Bothaina Kamel, 10/07/2011.

[37] Interview with Doaa Abdelaal, 27/07/2011.

[38] Interview with M.S., assistant to the Mufti, 24/06/2011.

[39] The current cabinet of Ganzory appointed the 8th of December 2011 changed some figures and included new faces, increasing the number of ministers. The cabinet includes 29 ministers, only two of which are women. A Consultative Council has been also appointed to assist SCAF in the coming period out of which only 30% are women.

[40] The new electoral law says that each proportional list must have at least one woman. Hence, parties that place women high on a list, particularly in

slots one to three, are pushing for having women elected. On the contrary, women at the very bottom of the list, have scarce possibilities of getting elected. In the majority of the party lists women are in the bottom half or bottom third of the lists. Occasionally, a woman is in high position. Only the Egyptian Social Democratic Party has candidated twenty-four women; also the Wafd Party has eighty-seven female candidates on the lists (Bowman 2011).

[41] Interview with Nehad Abol Komsan, 26/07/2011.

[42] Interview with Azza Kamel, 13/07/2011.

[43] Interview with Myriam Zaki, 22/06/2011.

[44] New Woman Foundation, Women and Memory Forum, Center of Egyptian Women Legal Aid, El Nadeem Center for the Rehabilitation of the Victims of Violence, Appropriate Communication Techniques for Development (ACT), Women's Forum for Development, Alliance of Arab Women, Egyptian Association for Family Development, "Nazra" Association for Feminist Studies, "Ommi" Association for Rights and Development, "Heya" Foundation.

[45] Interview with Dina Abou El Soud 06/07/2011.

[46] For a list of women groups that developed after the revolution and/or women's rights promoters, please see appendix n.2.

[47] See appendix n.3.

[48] On October 15, Hoda Badran, chairwoman of the AAW, together with 500 NGOs, launched the Egyptian Women Union. The union is expected to mobilize 1 million women during the elections and establish linkages with women in neighboring countries in the region.

[49] Interview with Mariz Tadros, 19/06/2011.

[50] Interview with Alia Dawood, 17/07/2011.

[51] This concept will be expanded in the concluding part.

[52] In 2007, the Brotherhood rejected certain provisions of the new Child Law, such as banning FGM and marriage below the age of eighteen, which were considered to be interferences with Islamic law.

[53] In previous documents, there was no specific mention about the position of women as head of state; rather, they declared that women were allowed to occupy all posts except for *al-imama al-kubra* (Abdel Latif 1, 2008).

[54] After the revolution of 2011, several youth left the movement. The Egyptian Current (Al-Tiyyar Al-Masri) is a new group (not yet licensed) comprising younger former Brotherhood activists who participated in the revolution and who are calling for a civil state rather than a religious one (Sharp 9, 2011).

[55] In 2008, women were still not yet represented in any of the movement's two main power structures, the *Majlis al-Shura* (Shura Council) and *Maktab al-Irshad* (Guidance Bureau) (Abdel Latif 7, 2008).

[56] Interview with Sarah Mohammed, 25/06/2011.

[57] He was recently expelled from the party for declaring himself a presidential candidate.

[58] Naem Abu Ghadda, head of "Si el Said" ("the master" association), plans to establish a political party that will aim to recover men's strength and over-throw calls of liberation that were adopted by the former first lady and her affiliates to help women disobey their husbands under the pretext of "equal-ity" (Abu Sakin).

[59] Interview with Mohasen Saber, 22/07/2011.

[60] Sectarian clashes also happened between Muslims and Christians during the last few months. Thousands of Salafis held demonstrations to release a priest's wife, Camilia Shehata, who they say converted to Islam and is now being held by the Coptic Church. Later in May around twelve people were killed when Salafis had surrounded a church and demanded that those in-side to release Abeer Fakhry, a woman who supposedly converted to Islam (Al Masry al Youm, May 13, 2011).

[61] Please refer to the first chapter for a complete overview of the methodo-logical approach.

[62] It is interesting to note that one male member of the family, while listening to the focus group, interfered in the discussion, telling her that Shari'a law is elastic and that she needs to define what she means in terms of women's need of being supported by a man.

[63] A question from a Facebook group called المسلمين في مصر لا لحكم الإخوان was launched in April. The group is asking people if they support a woman for president or not. An overwhelming majority does not support a woman as resident. Updated on May 25: 21,883 voted 'yes' and 85,780 'no.'

[64] In some cases, participants diverged from their debates to discuss discrim-inatory laws, like those of the penal code. This happened in particular during the third focus group, in which Khaled argued about the unfair treatment of women in case of murder. However, for reasons of space, this issue cannot be reported here in all its length.

[65] Both the MB and the Salafis have recently established their new political parties. Here I am simply referring to them as groups, without distinguishing the political parties from the groups themselves.

[66] In the appendix, it is possible to find some of the key points drawn from the answers collected in the open space of the survey.

[67] I cannot report the remarkable experiences I had with all those with whom I had an interview. Each one of them will necessitate an entire chapter for the deep emotions and thoughts they have stirred up.

[68] It should be considered that this work only targeted a small percentage of Egyptians. The current elections underlined another reality, where the major-ity of the population has democratically elected Islamist forces to form the new Parliament.

[69] Only on those occasions in which women played politics, as Doria Shafik did in both 1951 and 1954, did women achieve concrete results. The hunger strike in protest of the denial of women's political rights led by Shafik, pushed the government of Nasser to consider the introduction of equal political

rights for women in the new Constitution of 1956.

[70] For more insights on this topic, kindly read chapter three.

[71] Presentation at UN Women conference: "Pathways for Women in Democratic Transitions: International Experiences and Lessons Learned" (Tadros 2011).

[72] Image of the woman harassed and stripped by army soldiers late in December 2011. Demonstration of women in protection of women's rights after the army's assault of women in December (Source: Google). Women and men show their support to Samira Ibrahim outside the State Council Administrative (Source: UN Women).

[73] References in brackets have been shortened for stylistic reasons. Please refer to the final bibliography for more details. Also note that this chronology only covers the main events that happened between January and August 2011. Many other minor events have not been inserted for space constraints.

[74] Events that begin in a new paragraph happened under the same date.

[75] The answers reported here represent a summary of those that have been frequently repeated.
Uncompleted and vague answers have not been taken into consideration.

[76] The answers are not stated in order of importance.

www.ingramcontent.com/pod-product-compliance
Lightning Source LLC
Chambersburg PA
CBHW051344280526
45784CB00007B/2812